Industrial Revolution

An Enthralling Look at How Machines and Factories Changed Our World

© Copyright 2025 - All rights reserved.

The content contained within this book may not be reproduced, duplicated, or transmitted without direct written permission from the author or the publisher.

Under no circumstances will any blame or legal responsibility be held against the publisher, or author, for any damages, reparation, or monetary loss due to the information contained within this book, either directly or indirectly.

Legal Notice:

This book is copyright protected. It is only for personal use. You cannot amend, distribute, sell, use, quote, or paraphrase any part, or the content within this book, without the consent of the author or publisher.

Disclaimer Notice:

Please note the information contained within this document is for educational and entertainment purposes only. All effort has been executed to present accurate, up-to-date, reliable, and complete information. No warranties of any kind are declared or implied. Readers acknowledge that the author is not engaging in the rendering of legal, financial, medical, or professional advice. The content within this book has been derived from various sources. Please consult a licensed professional before attempting any techniques outlined in this book.

By reading this document, the reader agrees that under no circumstances is the author responsible for any losses, direct or indirect, that are incurred as a result of the use of the information contained within this document, including, but not limited to, errors, omissions, or inaccuracies.

Free limited time bonus

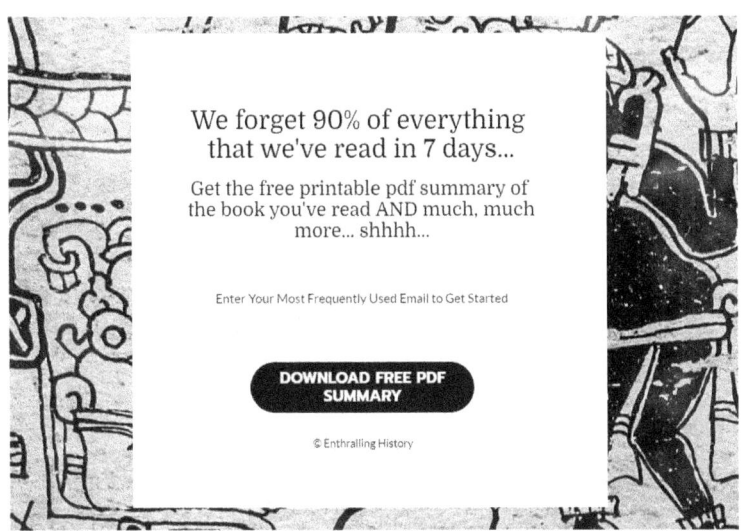

Stop for a moment. We have a free bonus set up for you. The problem is this: we forget 90% of everything that we read after 7 days. Crazy fact, right? Here's the solution: we've created a printable, 1-page pdf summary for this book that you're reading now. All you have to do to get your free pdf summary is to go to the following website: https://livetolearn.lpages.co/enthrallinghistory/

Or, Scan the QR code!

Once you do, it will be intuitive. Enjoy, and thank you!

Table of Contents

INTRODUCTION 1
CHAPTER 1: ENCLOSURE ACTS AND JETHRO TULL'S SEED DRILL...4
CHAPTER 2: JAMES WATT AND THE STEAM ENGINE 17
CHAPTER 3: RICHARD ARKWRIGHT'S WATER FRAME 30
CHAPTER 4: THE TRANSFORMATION OF THE TEXTILE INDUSTRY...39
CHAPTER 5: HENRY BESSEMER AND THE MASS PRODUCTION OF STEEL...53
CHAPTER 6: GEORGE STEPHENSON AND THE STEAM LOCOMOTIVE..61
CHAPTER 7: SAMUEL MORSE AND THE TELEGRAPH.............................72
CHAPTER 8: CHILD LABOR AND THE FACTORY ACTS 83
CHAPTER 9: SPREAD OF INDUSTRIALIZATION 94
CONCLUSION..99
HERE'S ANOTHER BOOK BY ENTHRALLING HISTORY THAT YOU MIGHT LIKE..102
FREE LIMITED TIME BONUS..103
BIBLIOGRAPHY 104
IMAGE SOURCES 113

Introduction

Writing on a computer, searching online for a book, downloading a book to your e-reader—these are all part of our daily life that we take for granted today. Who developed the technology that enabled you to read online? What inspired that person to do so?

Behind all of this technology is a long line of inventions and innovations that started with the Industrial Revolution. Spanning just over two centuries, the Industrial Revolution was the period of time when our society shifted from local, agrarian economies to the global industrialization we recognize today. Driven by inventions in machinery and a new factory-based system of work, the Industrial Revolution introduced a series of groundbreaking technological innovations in a relatively short period of time.

Originating in Great Britain, this era saw a rise in factories that were powered by coal and steam, as well as a massive societal shift as people were thrust into a whole new way of working. Some benefited greatly, like the factory owners and manufacturers, while others were forced to work in an increasingly exploitative labor market. People started moving away from their rural lives into cities as factories became the new norm and centralized production crossed industries. The Industrial Revolution boosted economic growth, contributing to the British Empire's dominance over international trade and colonization, but this prosperity was not always reflected equally. The use of cheap labor, even enslaved labor, helped to make those in control extremely wealthy while the working class struggled in poverty.

At the heart of this revolution was a series of groundbreaking inventions that fundamentally changed manufacturing and how people lived, many of them in the textile industry. With the introduction of James Hargreaves's spinning jenny in 1764, manual skilled labor suddenly became faster and more efficient. It involved more automation and less delicate work. This invention set off a snowball effect, as other machines—the spinning mule, water frame, and power loom—turned cloth-making from a cottage industry into a large-scale industrial operation. Perhaps the most famous invention was the steam engine. James Watt's improved steam engine in the 1760s unleashed the power of steam and coal, making the spinning machines even more powerful. The days of laboring intensively over spun yarn and hand-woven cloth disappeared as more and more factories opened up, employing people alongside machines that could produce a larger quantity of cloth than ever before. These machines could work day and night. They did not have to feed themselves or balance their production with farm work; they could run continuously, generating profit alongside product.

The factory system centralized production, bringing workers out of the home and under one roof. The system allowed for mass production and dramatically reduced the cost of goods, making them more accessible to the broader population. Of course, with innovation comes a cost, and for the factory system, that was the rise in cheap labor. Factory workers were often one step away from abject poverty. They were forced to live and work in close quarters and unsanitary conditions. Injury and disease ran rampant.

The revolution in manufacturing was complemented by developments in transportation and communication. The invention of the steam locomotive by George Stephenson revolutionized land transport and connected cities, leading to the growth of trade between them. These locomotives were adapted to carry people as well as goods, allowing British society to become more connected. The people experienced a period of freedom of movement that led to a shrinking world. Someone in Manchester could visit the sea in only a day, deliver a letter in the afternoon, or receive coal from a factory on a regular basis. When Samuel Morse invented the telegraph, the world shrank a little more as people could communicate across the world quicker than ever before, sharing news from across the seas in mere minutes.

However, the Industrial Revolution was not without its dark side. The rapid growth of factories led to exploitative labor practices, including the widespread use of child labor, leading to a whole generation with health complications and illiteracy. Children were often forced to work to supplement their parents' income. Working conditions were often dangerous and unhealthy, with long hours, low wages, and almost zero protections for those working. These issues and many more eventually led to labor reforms and the rise in workers' rights, but this did not happen until the effects of workers' exploitation had reached a critical point.

The Industrial Revolution also sparked a revolution in scientific and technological innovations. The increasing application of science to industry led to a cycle of discovery and invention. New materials like steel became central to industrial production, while new energy sources, such as electricity and petroleum, helped to power the next wave of technological advancement. As the Industrial Revolution spread from Britain to other parts of Europe and North America, it took on different characteristics. In the United States, for example, the revolution was marked by innovations like the cotton gin and the development of interchangeable parts in manufacturing, as well as the exploitation of enslaved people in the transatlantic slave trade. The spread of industrialization also fueled imperial ambitions, as industrialized nations sought new markets and sources of raw materials for their goods.

The legacy of the Industrial Revolution continues to shape our world today. The basic pattern of technological innovation driving economic and social change, which was established during this period, remains a fundamental part of modern economies. The challenges the revolution presented, from labor rights to environmental protections, continue to be important issues today. In essence, the Industrial Revolution was not just a period of technological change but also a fundamental reimagining of the relationship between humans, machines, and the natural world. It set in motion forces that continue to transform our society, economy, and environment to this day.

Chapter 1: Enclosure Acts and Jethro Tull's Seed Drill

Before the start of the Industrial Revolution, farming and agricultural practices were vastly different than how they are today, not only thanks to the machinery that was invented but also based on the distribution of land and the rotation of crops. Jethro Tull and his seed drill kickstarted the many mechanical innovations that changed the landscape of agriculture and farming, allowing for more productivity and better crop yields. The seed drill and the Enclosure Acts of Britain also began to change the fabric of British society, pushing people into the cities since less manual labor was needed on the farms.

Pre-Enclosure: The Open-Field System and Communal Agriculture

Before the 18th century, British agriculture operated under the open-field system, a medieval practice in which villages managed land communally. Large fields were divided into narrow strips that were farmed by peasant tenants, who paid rent or labor to the local lords. The fields followed a three-field rotation system in which two fields grew necessary crops like barley or wheat, and the third field stayed empty to restore the soil's fertility. Communal grazing lands, forests, and waterways provided the essentials for tenant farmers, allowing them to gather firewood for their homes, raise and feed their livestock, and harvest smaller shared crops.

While this system functioned for hundreds of years, by the beginning of the 18th century, it was starting to show its inefficiencies. The three-field rotation system limited flexibility and experimentation with crops, and the fragmented and confusing system of land ownership hindered the large-scale production and innovation of the agricultural industry. The system was built to cater to a local economy, and as the population of Britain began to expand, the agricultural industry faced more demand. Population growth and urbanization intensified the demand for food, and the constraints of the open-field system became more and more unsustainable.

The Enclosure Acts

The Enclosure Acts refer to parliamentary acts that slowly converted the open-field system into organized ("enclosed") parcels for private development. These acts, which began in 1604, privatized over 6.8 million acres of common land, stripping the peasants of their traditional rights to graze livestock, forage, and grow crops. Instead, the communal land was consolidated into privately managed farm plots overseen by a parish or lord.

In the beginning, land enclosures happened through informal agreements between landowners and tenant farmers. It wasn't until 1750 that enclosure by parliamentary acts became the norm.

The Enclosure Acts provided a legal framework and structure to convert common land into private property, clarify and strengthen property rights, and eliminate communal rights of land. The goal was to formalize and consolidate land ownership rights, which were seen as unclear and inefficient.

Timeline of the Enclosure Acts

1604: First Parliamentary Enclosure Act

- The Melcombe Regis and Radipole, Dorset (Church) Act marks the beginning of parliamentary enclosures. This allowed landowners to enclose the land as long as the whole community agreed to it, leading to the rise of "piecemeal enclosure," where enclosures would happen through private arrangements and informal agreements.

1607: The Midland Revolt

- This was a popular uprising that occurred in the Midlands (Northamptonshire, Warwickshire, and Leicestershire) in response to the enclosure of common lands. This early example of popular protest involved approximately nine thousand people at its peak and led to increased scrutiny over the social impact of enclosures, particularly the depopulation of the land.

1624: Enclosure of Gillingham Forest

- This marked a shift in state policy toward supporting enclosures as economic goods.

1633-1660: Cromwellian Era

- Enclosures accelerated during this period, with reduced legal obstacles following the abolition of the Star Chamber in 1641.

1650: The Diggers' Movement

- During the English Civil War (1642-1651), a radical group led by Gerard Winstanley challenged the enclosure system by occupying and cultivating common lands in Surrey. They argued against private enclosure, stating that the earth should be a "common treasury." The movement was quickly suppressed by landowners, but it was a major influence on later debates on land rights.

1755-1773: Inclosure (or Enclosure) Act

- This was part of the first major wave of parliamentary enclosures. The Inclosure Act of 1773 established a more standardized process for enclosure, removing commoners' access rights.

1760-1840: Draining of Fens

- Parliamentary acts authorized the large-scale drainage and enclosure of the Fens, a vast marshy lowland in eastern England. This process converted wetlands into productive agricultural land through the construction of drainage channels, embankments, and sluices. The transformation significantly boosted agricultural output but disrupted traditional local livelihoods. The introduction of steam power around 1840 accelerated the final stages of this massive land reclamation project.

1801: General Enclosure Act

- This act simplified the enclosure process, allowing landowners to enclose land without individual parliamentary acts as long as 75 percent of the landowners agreed.

1836: Tithe Act

- The Tithe Act mandated the commutation (changing how you get paid from something) of tithe payments to rent charges, which impacted the enclosure process.

1845: Inclosure Act

- This act appointed permanent Inclosure commissioners with the power to approve enclosures without parliamentary submission, meaning they didn't have to get approval from Parliament first.

1876: Commons Act

- The Commons Act was enacted in 1876, slowing down the Enclosure Movement by protecting common land.

1899: Board of Agriculture Takes Over

- The Board (later Ministry) of Agriculture and Fisheries assumed the powers of the Inclosure commissioners.

1914: Final Enclosure Act

- The last parliamentary enclosure act was passed in 1914, marking the end of a three-hundred-year process that privatized nearly all of England's common land. This final act formalized the transition from communal to private land ownership, concluding a chapter that reshaped rural landscapes, agricultural practices, and social structures.

Over 5,200 individual enclosure acts were passed between 1604 and 1914; this number does not include a number of informal agreements that led to enclosures in the early years of the process. By the end, enclosure was the norm and had transformed British agriculture and labor. The Agricultural Revolution, facilitated by the Enclosure Acts, contributed to increased efficiency and productivity. There were greater crop yields, and many technological innovations were introduced that contributed to the Industrial Revolution as a whole. At the same time, these acts displaced small farmers and peasants.

The Enclosure Movement led to great social upheaval, but it also innovated farming. Thanks to the enclosure system, the Norfolk four-course system replaced the three-field rotation system in farming, boosting grain yields and helping to sustain larger herds (which, in turn, created larger manure supplies for fertilization). The privatization of land also created incentives for landowners to improve the infrastructure on and around their enclosed parcels and to more carefully consider how their crops were planted, leading to scientific innovations in breeding and soil management.

Social Upheaval and the Enclosure System

The Enclosure Acts meant the end of the open-field system, where peasants shared common land for cultivation and subsistence. The common lands were redistributed to private landowners, who put up fences and other barriers that prevented communal use. This led to the displacement of rural families who had relied on the common lands for their livelihood. Many rural communities disintegrated as villagers left their homes, leading to the mass migration of people from rural areas to the cities, where they sought employment in factories instead. In the long run, the Enclosure Acts enabled economic and technological growth, but they also exacerbated social inequality, reorganizing class structures and causing unemployment or poverty for most of the English population who were not part of the ruling or aristocratic class.

The peasants and tenant farmers did not succumb to the new social structure without a fight. Protests like the Midland Revolt and the Diggers' Movement show us that there were many who saw the inequality for what it was and fought for a more equal distribution of land.

The Goose and the Common

In 1821, during the height of the Enclosure Movement, an anonymous poem was published in a magazine, highlighting the attitudes toward the upheaval of the Enclosure Movement.

"The law locks up the man or woman
Who steals the goose from off the common
But leaves the greater villain loose
Who steals the common from off the goose.

The law demands that we atone
When we take things we do not own
But leaves the lords and ladies fine
Who take things that are yours and mine.

The poor and wretched don't escape
If they conspire the law to break;
This must be so but they endure
Those who conspire to make the law.
The law locks up the man or woman

Who steals the goose from off the common
And geese will still a common lack
Till they go and steal it back."
- Anonymous[i]

This anonymous poem is deeply rooted in the feelings of resentment caused by the privatization of common lands in England, and it serves as a critique of the Enclosure Acts. It highlights the injustice of a system that allows wealthy landowners to appropriate traditionally communal resources while punishing the poor who had relied on the common lands for subsistence. It shows us that the Enclosure Acts were not passed without resistance, and that while they led to significant economic growth, they also caused growing pains within the working-class population. The poem's relevance has continued into the 21st century and is often quoted in discussions about the privatization of other common resources.

The legal and economic motivations for enclosure reflect the changing priorities of 18th- and 19th-century England. As the country moved toward industrialization and capitalist agriculture, the traditional system of communal land use was seen as an obstacle to progress. The Enclosure Acts provided a legal mechanism to overcome this obstacle, aligning property rights with the economic goals of increased productivity and profit. The debate over whether enclosure was a necessary step in agricultural modernization or an unjust appropriation of communal resources continues to this day, highlighting the complex interplay between legal, economic, and social factors in shaping land use policies.

Economic Motivations of the Enclosure Acts

The Enclosure Acts provided compelling economic motivations for landowners of the time. Enclosed land was promoted as being more productive, allowing farmers to adopt more efficient practices without the constraints and disorganization of communal management. This land was seen as crucial for feeding an expanding population. Landowners sought to maximize rental income from their estates since enclosed land could command higher rents from tenant farmers. Also, by consolidating scattered strips of land into enclosed farms, farmers were able to adopt

---

[i] Conner, Clifford D. "The Goose on the Common." Science for the People Magazine, vol. 24, no. 3, Science for the People, www.magazine.scienceforthepeople.org/vol24-3-cooperation/the-goose-on-the-common/. Accessed 3 Feb. 2025.

new crop management techniques. The economic motivation wasn't exclusive to agricultural production (though that is what we've been focusing on); enclosure also allowed landowners to protect mineral deposits and other natural resources that would be used during industrialization.

As part of a broader economic strategy, policymakers saw enclosure as a means to shift domestic production priorities and support industrialization as England's colonial reach expanded. High grain prices, particularly during the Napoleonic Wars (late 18th-early 19th century), encouraged landowners to invest in enclosure to maximize profits. In periods of high inflation, landowners were motivated to borrow and invest in enclosure since inflation would reduce the real cost of loan repayments over time.

New Farming Techniques: The Norfolk Four-Course Rotation

The Norfolk four-course rotation system was developed in the early 16th century in present-day Belgium and was popularized in the 18th century by British agriculturalist Charles Townshend. It involved a four-year cycle of crops: wheat, turnips, barley, and either clover or ryegrass. In the first year of the rotation, wheat was grown; in the second, turnips (which served as winter feed for livestock); in the third year, barley, with clover and ryegrass undersown, a process that reduces soil erosion in winter months; and finally, in the fourth year, clover and ryegrass were either grazed by livestock or cut for feed. The four crops would be planted in four fields, so there was always wheat, barley, turnips, and clover/ryegrass planted on the farm. This was revolutionary for farmers since they could now maintain larger herds throughout the year. The livestock could feed on either turnips, clover, or ryegrass, so farmers didn't have to slaughter their livestock before winter due to the lack of fodder.

The cumulative effects of the system resulted in a huge increase in productivity. The fodder crops (turnips, clover, and ryegrass) were consumed by livestock and produced a large and consistent amount of animal manure, which was richer than before thanks to the animals' improved diet. When sheep grazed in the fields, their waste fertilized the soil, promoting even larger cereal yields in subsequent years. The increase in soil fertility and easier access to manure were crucial since they allowed for continuous cultivation without depleting the soil's nutrients.

The success of the Norfolk four-course system sparked a wider adoption of crop rotation techniques, and modern variations of the four-course system are still in use today. A contemporary version of the wheat-turnip-barley-clover rotation might include peas, field beans, wheat, potatoes, or barley as part of the four crops in rotation. The new farming techniques of the Agricultural Revolution allowed for greater food productivity, which supported Britain's growing population and a shift in the labor force. This surplus of food and labor enabled the technological advances of the Industrial Revolution.

Jethro Tull: Agricultural Pioneer

While his name may be better associated with a '70s rock band, Jethro Tull was a British agriculturalist and inventor. He was born in 1674 in Berkshire, England, into a family of gentlemen. His early life was marked by a privileged upbringing with a strong emphasis on education. In 1699, Tull attended Oxford University, where he studied law and became a member of Gray's Inn, where he was called to the bar. It's likely that Tull set out for a career in law and politics, as was suitable at the time, but his life would take an unexpected turn after he fell ill with a pulmonary disorder. It was around this time that he married Susanna Smith and began working on his father's farm at Howberry in Oxfordshire.

The health setback led him away from the legal profession. Rather than sit for the bar, Tull toured Europe while recovering, settling for a while in Montpellier, France. There, he observed the agricultural practices in France, comparing them to those in Britain and Italy. It broadened his perspective and expanded his understanding of farming beyond what he had learned while working on his father's farm. Upon returning to England in 1709, Tull took charge of a farm called Prosperous in Shalbourne (then in Berkshire but now part of Wiltshire).

Observations on Seed Sowing

Tull's observations of manual seed sowing during his European tour played a crucial role in inspiring his later invention. During his time in southern France and Italy, Tull observed and compared the agricultural practices of the regions. In Lombardy, Tull noted how farmers planted beans in rows—a practice that was different from the traditional broadcast sowing method in England (where a laborer scattered seeds across the field as they walked). In the French Languedoc region, Tull observed vineyard workers breaking the soil between the vines and constantly hoeing weeds. This practice of continuous soil cultivation impressed him and led him to develop the theory that penetration by air, water, and nutrients was essential to improve soil fertility. When he acquired Prosperous Farm in 1709, he began to apply these observations to his own farming practices. As he started to recognize the inefficiencies of broadcast seed sowing, which often led to uneven seed distribution, wasted seeds, or overcrowding, he became inspired to develop the seed drill.

The Seed Drill: A Revolutionary Farming Tool

Tull invented the seed drill in 1701. This was a mechanical device designed to plant seeds at regular intervals and at a consistent depth. Tull named his invention a "drill" because farmers traditionally referred to the action of sowing beans and peas into channels or furrows by hand as "drilling."

The seed drill incorporated several key features that were inspired by his European observations:

- Row planting: The machine sowed seeds in neat, equally spaced rows, similar to the bean planting he had seen in Lombardy.
- Precise depth control: Seeds were planted at a consistent depth, ensuring better germination rates.
- Efficient seed use: The drill reduced seed waste by precisely placing seeds rather than scattering them by hand.
- The use of horses: The wide spacing between rows allowed for horse-drawn implements to cultivate the soil between plants, which was inspired by the vineyard practices he observed in France.

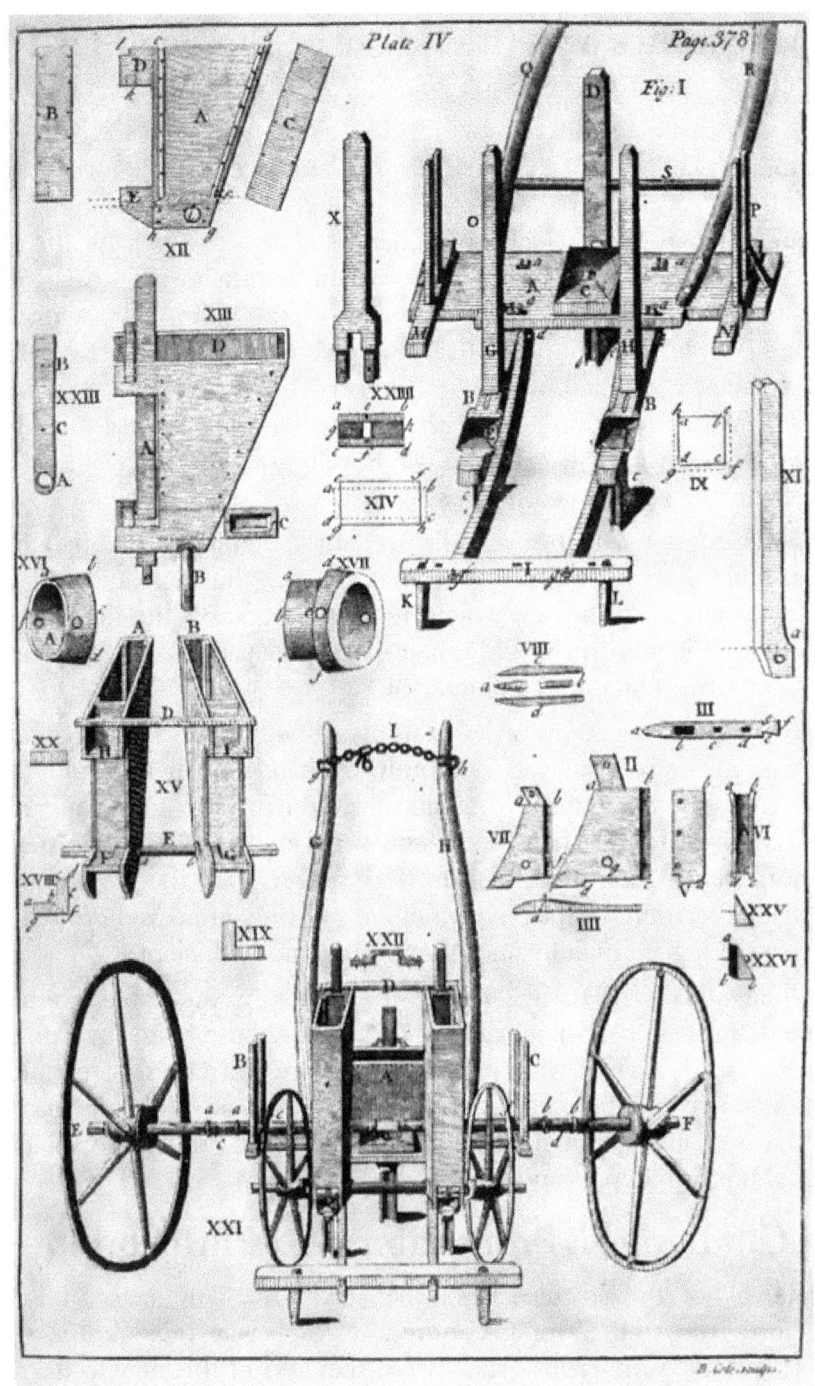

Jethro Tull's seed drill.[1]

Mechanics and the Usage of the Seed Drill

The seed drill was a complex yet ingenious machine composed of several interconnected components. At its core was a large hopper positioned at the top of the device, which stored the seeds for planting. Beneath the hopper was a precisely engineered rotating cylinder with carefully cut grooves, which controlled seed distribution. As the drill moved across the field, this cylinder would turn, allowing seeds to fall into its carefully designed channels. A funnel positioned below the rotating cylinder guided the seeds downward into the soil. At the front of the machine, a specialized plow created narrow furrows into which the seeds would be deposited. The harrow attached to the rear of the device immediately covered the planted seeds with soil, protecting them and ensuring proper germination.

Farmers would prepare the seed drill by filling its hopper with seeds, typically wheat, barley, or other grains. The machine was then hitched to a team of horses, which would pull it across the field. As the horses moved, the drill would create perfectly spaced rows, depositing seeds at a consistent depth and interval.

This was a dramatic improvement over traditional broadcast sowing, where seeds were scattered randomly by hand. Farmers could plant three rows simultaneously, dramatically reducing the time and labor required for planting. The wide spacing between rows allowed farmers to use horse-drawn cultivating tools to weed and manage the crops without damaging the young plants. This method not only improved crop yields but also made field maintenance significantly more efficient.

While initially met with skepticism, Tull's invention was gradually adopted throughout Britain and improved over the years by farmers. Today's seed drills, while benefiting from advanced technology, fundamentally operate on Tull's original innovation. The technology may have changed, but the core purpose remains the same: planting seeds at uniform depths and intervals.

Challenges, Promotion, and Philosophy

Despite all of the advantages of the seed drill, Tull faced a lot of resistance from the farming community, especially the laborers who sowed and tilled the crops. Many were skeptical of this new technology and reluctant to change their traditional methods. Some even feared that the machine would take away their jobs. Undeterred, Tull continued to refine his invention over the years and continued promoting his innovative farming techniques. He conducted experiments on his own farm, writing about the effectiveness of his methods. In a bold move to prove the superiority of his approach, Tull is reported to have cultivated crops without manure for over a decade, relying solely on his seed drill and other innovations. Tull also developed an improved plow that allowed for the continuous cultivation of the same field over multiple years, challenging the old practice of the three-field crop rotation system and promoting the Norfolk four-course rotation.

In 1732, Tull published his magnum opus, *Horse-Hoeing Husbandry*, an essay that detailed his farming techniques, machines, and agricultural philosophy. The essay initially faced a lot of criticism, but gradually, Tull's essay gained widespread recognition for his innovative ideas, including Tull's new method of cultivation that used the seed drill and the horse-drawn hoe.

Tull's innovations went far beyond machinery. He advocated for a scientific approach to farming, emphasizing the importance of soil cultivation and challenging traditional beliefs about fertilization. Tull correctly theorized that plants needed to be spaced farther apart and that the soil around them should be broken down and loosened during growth, which would help the plants grow better during sowing and in the early stages of root development.

The essay's influence traveled far, having been read and championed by American figures like George Washington and Thomas Jefferson. *Horse-Hoeing Husbandry* is now a cornerstone of agricultural literature and is still considered relevant in modern times. The essay has been translated into multiple languages and continues to be studied for its role in innovating farming, especially in regard to tillage, soil management, and efficiency.

Jethro Tull died in 1741 at Prosperous Farm. He was buried in the graveyard of St. Bartholomew's Church in Lower Basildon, Berkshire, which you can still visit today. The impact of Jethro Tull's work extended far beyond his lifetime and can be considered the basis for the Industrial Revolution that followed. The efficiencies in planting, combined with Britain's new enclosure system, provided enough food to sustain a growing population, and it also provided a new workforce for the industrial innovations that would soon follow. Tull's seed drill was the first step in the mechanization of farming and agriculture, and the principles he established—namely, precision planting, efficient seed usage, and science-led cultivation methods—became a fundamental part of farming.

Shift from Agricultural to Industrial Labor

As agricultural productivity improved through innovations like the Norfolk four-course rotation and Jethro Tull's seed drill, as well as the consequences of the Enclosure Acts, fewer workers were needed to produce food for the wider population. By the mid-19th century, more people were living in towns and cities than in rural areas. This was driven by the rise in factories, which promised more stability to the displaced farm laborers.

The peasants weren't the only members of the population who moved out of the country and into the city. Thanks to mechanization, the children of more successful farmers could branch out and begin to seek their fortunes elsewhere without needing to be called back to the farm to help. This shift fueled the growth of Britain's trade markets and created new occupations. As the labor force moved from the farms to the factories, industrialization grew, leading to the rapid expansion of factories and mines across the country.

Chapter 2: James Watt and the Steam Engine

Following the Agricultural Revolution, Britain was now free to take a leap in energy production and industrialization, and at its core was the steam engine. Steam power has a long history, but in 1769, James Watt refined and revolutionized the steam engine into the productive and powerful machine that changed transportation, the textile industry, and countless other industries.

The History of Steam Power

The use of steam power spans over two thousand years, with its roots stretching back to ancient times. The first recorded steam engine was the aeolipile, which dates back between 30 and 15 BCE in writings by the ancient Roman architect and engineer Vitruvius. It was later described by Heron of Alexandria in 1st-century Roman Egypt. It wasn't until the 17th and 18th centuries, however, that steam power began to take on a new and more powerful form.

Timeline of Steam-Powered Engines

30-15 BCE / 1st Century CE: The Aeolipile

- Vitruvius, a Roman architect and engineer, developed the aeolipile, an early steam device.
- In 1st century Roman Egypt, Heron of Alexandria (mathematician and engineer) described the device as a simple steam turbine consisting of a hollow sphere mounted on a

stand. The sphere could rotate freely, with two tubes attached to opposite sides of its widest point. When water inside the sphere was heated, steam would escape through the tubes, causing the sphere to spin. This device was not a practical machine for power generation, but it is an example of early steam innovation.

1679: Denis Papin Steam Digester
- Denis Papin invented the pressure cooker, which was designed to extract fat from bone in high-pressure steam environments. This early pressure cooker included a safety valve in a cylinder-and-piston design, which inspired later steam pressure machines.

1698: Thomas Savery's Atmospheric Pressure Engine
- This was the first practical steam engine for pumping water from mines. It used atmospheric pressure and steam condensation to extract water. Savery was inspired by Papin's cylinder design.

1712: Thomas Newcomen's Atmospheric Engine
- This was primarily used for pumping water from mines. These engines were installed across Britain and helped increase efficiency in British coal mines.
- Newcomen and others continued to make improvements to the atmospheric engine throughout the early 1700s.

1764: James Watt's Steam Engine
- James Watt patented his own steam engine, which was based on Newcomen's design and subsequent improvements.
- Watt's engine included a separate condenser, improving the efficiency of the machine, and a steam jacket and vacuum pump. It used the double-acting principle to the machine's advantage. (The double-acting principle states that pressure applied to a confined fluid acts equally in all directions.)
- 1775: Boulton and Watt's partnership led to the commercialization of Watt's steam engine. It is adopted across various industries.

- Watt continued to make improvements, adding the double-acting engine in 1782, which allowed steam to act on both sides of the piston.

1800-1850: Adoption of Steam Engines and the Industrial Revolution

- Richard Trevithick built the first steam-powered locomotive in 1803.
- In 1858, the maiden voyage of Brunel's SS *Great Eastern* took place. It was the largest steam-powered liner of the 19th century.
- Steam replaced water and wind power in many industries across Britain and, later, the world.

1869: Opening of the Suez Canal

- Steamships became the predominant sailing vessels on the newly opened trading route.

1897: Steam Cars: Personalization of Steam Power

- Steam Cars were automobiles that were powered by steam instead of fossil fuels. A steam car burned fuel that heated water in a boiler. This process generated steam that expanded and pushed pistons, which, in turn, turned a crankshaft, much like steam engines on locomotives.

    The first steam-powered automobile was created in 1815 by the Czech-Polish engineer and inventor Josef Božek. In the following years, steam cars were produced by various companies in the United States and Canada until 1930. Initially, steam cars were popular with consumers since steam was seen as safe, reliable, and familiar. However, these cars also took at least thirty minutes to start and required constant care. As automotive technology advanced, steam cars dramatically fell out of favor with consumers.

1903: Fisk Generating Station

- This station was built in Chicago, USA. It used steam-powered turbine generators for energy production.

1923: Release of "An Aerodynamic Theory of Turbine Design"

- This paper was written by Alan Arnold Griffith and helped improve steam turbine efficiency.

1933: First Steam-Powered Aircraft
- The Besler steam-driven plane had its first successful flight on April 12th, 1933, at Oakland Airport (in California, USA).

1938: The *Mallard* Sets a Record
- The *Mallard*, a steam train, set a world record for speed at 126 mph (203 km/h) in 1938

2009: British Steam Car Challenge
- On August 25th, 2009, the British Steam Car set a new record for land speed at 139.84 mph (225 kph).

Thomas Savery's Steam Engine

Descriptions and theories of utilizing steam power continued from the time of Vitruvius and Heron of Alexandria right up to the 17th century, when Thomas Savery developed a practical machine to harness steam power. Thomas Savery was born at Shilstone in Devon around 1650. He worked as a military engineer. Aside from his duties as a captain, Savery spent his time performing mechanical experiments. He took out patents for a variety of machines, from a device for polishing glass and marble to one that improved the efficiency of rowing ships. In 1698, using principles from Denis Papin's steam digester, Savery invented the first commercially used steam-powered pump, now known as the Savery Engine. His pump was primarily designed as a solution for draining water from coal mines.

The Savery engine consisted of a closed vessel filled with water. Pressurized steam was introduced into the vessel, forcing the water to reach a higher level. When the water was expelled, a sprinkler at the top of the machine condensed the remaining steam, creating a vacuum effect that drew up more water through a valve below.

While it was a groundbreaking and practical invention, it had many limitations. The machine had a limited pumping height, which made it impractical for use in the deep coal mines without installing multiple pumps on top of each other. The machine was also bulky and difficult to install in coal mines. It operated at very high pressures, making it prone to explosions, and it was not fitted with a safety valve. The combination of a lack of safety features and explosive risk factors made it too dangerous to use in the coal mines. There were also frequent failures and leaks in the machine.

The Savery engine required constant maintenance and an extremely large boiler in order to even function properly, once again proving it had limited use for its intended purpose of pumping water out of coal mines. It also required a lot of coal to power the large boilers, making it costly to run and inefficient for use anywhere that didn't have ready access to coal.

Despite these limitations, Savery continued to promote his invention for use in coal mines and to pump water into factories. It was the blueprint for steam-powered machines until 1712 when Thomas Newcomen introduced his own steam engine.

Thomas Newcomen and His Atmospheric Engine

Thomas Newcomen was born in 1664 in Dartmouth, Devon, to a family of merchants. He served as an apprentice engineer and began working as an ironmonger in 1685, specializing in the design and manufacturing of tools for the mining industry. Newcomen became familiar with the issue of flooding in British mines through his connections with a mine owner in Cornwall, who expressed the same problem that Savery had tried to fix. As mines were getting deeper, it was getting harder to remove water from them as traditional methods were inefficient and increasingly expensive. Inspired by this common problem, Newcomen began work on his own steam-powered pumping machine.

Working with his apprentice, John Calley (sources differ on whether he was a glazier or a plumber), Newcomen developed a new design for a steam engine based on the designs of Denis Papin. As neither Newcomen nor Calley was educated in mechanical engineering, they corresponded with Robert Hooke, a physicist, astronomer, geologist, and architect. Hooke was not supportive of their plan, but Newcomen and Calley persisted in their experiments. In 1698, they developed a steam engine prototype: a seven-inch-wide brass cylinder sealed with a leather flap around the edge of the piston—it was similar to Savery's engine. Newcomen's machine also operated by using steam to create a vacuum inside a cylinder. The weight of the atmosphere depressed a piston above, generating continuous power.

While Newcomen's engine was an improvement on Savery's, it still had several inefficiencies. It still used vast quantities of coal, again making it efficient only where coal was abundant and cheap; this meant the atmospheric engine was not adaptable outside of the mining industry.

The engine needed to be repeatedly heated and cooled, and it didn't transfer heat very well, which reduced the overall efficiency of the machine and was the reason why it needed so much coal. Also, the steam pressure and vacuum were very limited, meaning the engine could not provide very much power. It was enough to pump water out of mines but not enough to make the engine useful for other industries. Finally, while the components were more stable than Savery's engine, the Newcomen atmospheric engine had an uneven path of motion, which caused significant wear and tear on its components and required consistent maintenance. Newcomen continued to work on the engine, making improvements to the mechanics throughout his life.

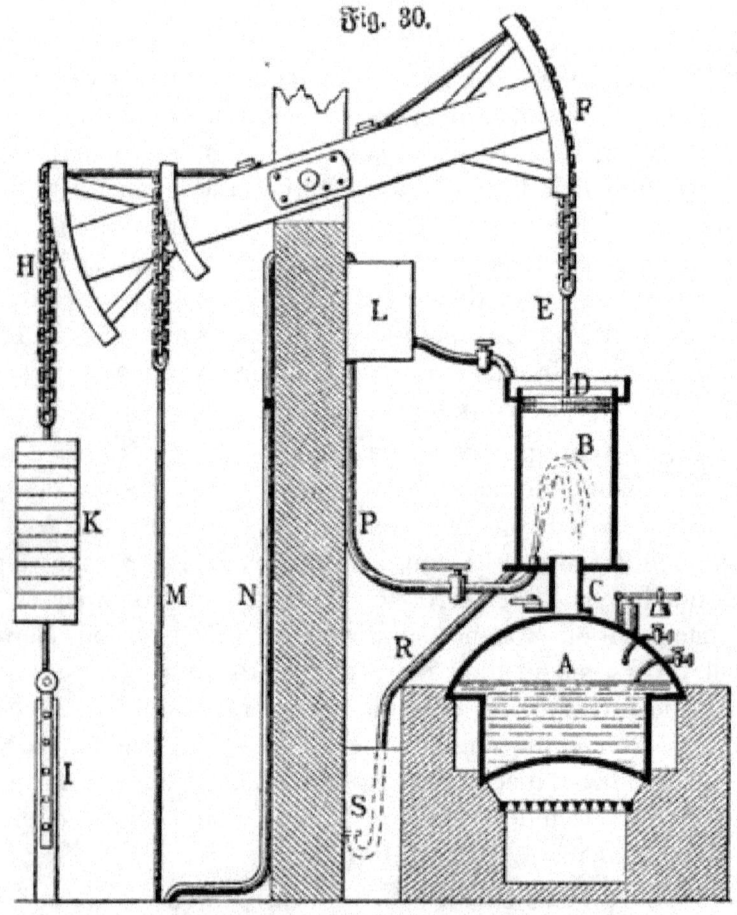

The Newcomen atmospheric engine.[1]

Despite all of its inefficiencies, the Newcomen engine was significantly more successful than the Savery engine, with over one hundred of them installed by 1735 and an estimated two thousand in operation by 1800. His atmospheric engine played a crucial role in enabling deeper mining operations across Britain and providing more fuel to the burgeoning industries across the country. It was the basis for Watt's steam engine, which revolutionized transport and manufacturing in the 19th century.

James Watt: Inventor of the Modern Steam Engine

James Watt was born on January 19th, 1736, in Greenock, Scotland, to a prominent family. His father was a carpenter, often working on the local steamships that had begun to come through Greenock. He was also the local treasurer and magistrate. Watt grew up surrounded by shipbuilders and merchants, and he reportedly read every book he could get his hands on. Due to ill health as a child, Watt was unable to attend the Greenock Grammar School and was instead taught at home by his mother. His poor constitution also led to Watt being exposed to his father's shipbuilding and carpentry business from a young age. Although he did not receive a consistent formal education, he was taught about the business that would make him famous later in his life: mechanics. At the age of seventeen, he moved to London to pursue a career as a mathematical instrument maker. After one year, he returned to Scotland, establishing a workshop at the University of Glasgow.

Workshop Experiments at the University of Glasgow

Watt established his workshop at the University of Glasgow in 1757, where he repaired and manufactured precision instruments like quadrants (used to measure angles in navigation and mathematics) and compasses, just as his father did before him. The university provided him with a room and a workshop, and his proficient skills earned him a small wage. All of this enabled James Watt to collaborate with prominent scientists at the University of Glasgow. British physicist and chemist Joseph Black taught at the university and introduced Watt to the scientific concept of latent heat.

In 1763, Watt was asked to repair a model of Thomas Newcomen's atmospheric engine. In his workshop, he identified various inefficiencies in the design. Watt conducted a number of experiments to understand what was going on. For example, he measured the amount of steam required to heat cold water to its boiling point, leading him to realize that latent heat was essential to the engine's efficient operation. His key insight was that the cylinder needed to remain as hot as the steam that entered it and that the condensation processes needed to happen below 37.8°C (100°F) in order to maximize the engine's power. This realization led Watt to develop the separate condenser. This kept the condenser away from the cylinder, which allowed the cylinder to stay hot from the latent heat of the steam. The condensation process could occur at a lower temperature in a separate part of the engine.

In addition to his work on the engine itself, James Watt also conducted experiments using a kettle and a glass tube in order to better understand the behavior of steam and even tried to build a model steam engine.

Fun Fact: The international unit of power, the watt (W), is named after James Watt in honor of his contributions to power generation.

James Watt's Steam Engine

James Watt's steam engine functioned the same as the Newcomen engine that came before it. However, Watt made four key improvements that allowed his engine to be more efficient.

- Separate Condenser: Watt's experiments helped him find the fundamental flaw in Newcomen's design. Instead of cooling and reheating the main cylinder with each stroke, which wasted energy, Watt created a separate chamber for condensing the steam. This allowed the main chamber to maintain its temperature and have the steam enter the chamber when it was still hot, dramatically improving the machine's efficiency.

- Double-Acting Engine: Newcomen's engine used steam to push the piston in only one direction and relied on atmospheric pressure for the return stroke. Watt developed a new system where steam powered both directions of the piston's movement, effectively doubling the engine's power output.

- Parallel Motion: Watt invented a series of linkages that adapted the piston's binary up-and-down motion into rotary motion while maintaining a straight line of movement. This expanded the engine's applications beyond its use in pumping water for mining operations.

- Centrifugal Governor: Watt added a device that regulated the engine's speed, providing a more consistent and reliable power output. The automatic control system used rotating weights to sense the engine's speed and adjusted the steam valve accordingly. When the engine ran too fast, the weights would rise and reduce the flow of steam; when it was too slow, the weights would drop and increase the flow of steam, ensuring a steady output of power.

These improvements transformed Newcomen's steam engine into a more practical and versatile power source, one that would drive the Industrial Revolution forward. Watt's design made steam power more economical than it had ever been before.

A Watt steam engine.⁹

Boulton & Watt: Marketing the Steam Engine

In 1769, James Watt applied for his first patent regarding the steam engine: No.913, "A New Invented Method of Lessening the Consumption of Steam and Fuel in Fire Engines." At the time of application, he only had a model of the engine based on his experiments, and the patent office granted him a period of four months to file for a specification. This was a process unique to the time period in which an inventor was given a period of time after his preliminary patent was approved to write a detailed document describing how the invention worked, often with technical drawings to complement the description.

During this period, Watt's initial partner, John Roebuck, who had agreed to finance the production of Watt's steam engine and had been financially supporting Watt during his experiments, faced bankruptcy after some poor business decisions. As a result, Watt struggled to bring his machine into production. Not only were his steam engines large and costly to produce by himself, but he also feared what could happen if someone copied his design and beat him to the market. He petitioned Parliament to extend the typical timeframe of his patent in 1775. In an unprecedented move, Parliament granted Watt an extension, the Fire Engine Act of 1775. Watt was given twenty-five years to continue to develop his machine, giving him enough time to continue to develop his invention and—crucially—find a new patron to finance production.

And here was where Matthew Boulton entered the picture. He was born in 1728 in Birmingham, England, and became a prominent English manufacturer, engineer, and entrepreneur. Boulton joined his family's metal business at a young age, becoming a partner in the business at the age of twenty-one. In 1775, after John Roebuck went bankrupt, Boulton offered to pay £1,200 for Roebuck's share in the patent, recognizing its revolutionary potential. Boulton helped to petition Parliament to grant an extension of Watt's patent, and he was also the one who could put money into the development and production of Watt's steam engine.

This partnership proved to be transformative. Matthew Boulton provided money, contacts, and business acumen to complement Watt's technological expertise and creativity. With Boulton's support, Watt was able to revisit and perfect his steam engine prototype. In 1776, the first successful Watt engine was produced at Boulton's Soho Manufactory in Birmingham. The partnership went on to install hundreds of Boulton & Watt steam engines throughout Britain and abroad.

Throughout all of this, the firm of Boulton & Watt turned itself into a hub of innovation as the company supported other talents and inventors, even opening the patent to others who wanted to improve upon Watt's initial invention.

Soho Manufactory

As the partnership flourished, the two men realized they needed somewhere to produce the machine. The pair established Soho Manufactory in Birmingham. It was the first to produce the steam engine and later became a center of innovation. After years in the Soho Manufactory, the pair opened Soho Foundry in 1796, which was created as a dedicated facility for manufacturing steam engines.

Boulton and Watt established standardized, interchangeable machine parts, which simplified stock and repairs for their machines. They broke down the various parts of production and elements of the machine, creating specialized tasks so that it was possible to work on more than one machine at a time. They also organized the workshops within the factory to optimize their workflow. This method of building machines was improved over a hundred years later with Henry Ford and his production line.

In addition to revolutionizing the workshops, they also set up detailed accounting procedures, with separate profit centers for the different departments within Soho Manufactory. The two were known to have a very progressive management style and provided welfare for their workers by creating a safe, comfortable working environment and providing for their employees in times of financial need. They were very ahead of their time, reflecting concepts (like Ford's production line) that would only become common in the world of manufacturing and invention a century later. It also allowed the pair to continue developing new innovations alongside marketing the steam engine.

The marketing strategies used by Boulton and Watt were crucial for promoting the steam engine across various industries. They knew the steam engine could be used for other industries besides coal mining, so they needed to find ways that would make the engine seem universal rather than another coal mine engine. One of the most enduring innovations was the concept of "horsepower," a metric that compared the output of a steam engine to a team of horses working together. The concept was invented by Watt and eventually became a global standard. Comparing steam engine output to a team of horses brought a sense of familiarity to the new machine and proved to be a persuasive marketing tool.

From the beginning, the pair aimed to establish themselves as the leading producer of steam engines in Britain. Their efforts to promote the machine ensured that the Watt steam engine was quickly adopted in industries that had previously not made use of steam power, like the textile industry (which was beginning its transition into mechanics with power looms and the water frame) and breweries. Boulton and Watt published technical booklets for their customers, providing detailed descriptions of the operation and mechanics of the engines.

The Watt Patent Cases

Matthew Boulton and James Watt aggressively defended their patents against competitors to the point where many historians now see it as a suppressive action to make sure their machine reigned supreme. This can best be seen in their actions against inventor Jonathan Hornblower. Hornblower had developed a compound steam engine with multiple cylinders that was more efficient than Watt's design. It was more technologically advanced than Watt's and would become more popular once Watt's patent expired in 1800. However, Boulton and Watt managed to block Hornblower's attempts at getting a patent because his design incorporated Watt's separate condenser.

This pattern of using elements of Watt's design to suppress other inventors and block their patents was repeated multiple times. Edward Bull was sued in 1793 for infringing on the patent by using a separate condenser. John Wilkinson mounted approximately twenty engines without express permission from Boulton and Watt (doing so on the belief that they were friends) and was sued in 1796. Matthew Wasborough's crank motion design was blocked by Watt as well. These patent cases always forced the opposing party to settle with Boulton and Watt, sometimes (as in the case with Jonathan Hornblower) sending them into financial ruin.

Boulton and Watt achieved their goal of steam engine supremacy in Britain, but at what cost? During the period of Watt's patent protection, which lasted until 1800, steam engines were adopted at a rate of about 750 engines per year throughout the United Kingdom. In the decades after the patent expired, this figure blew up to over four thousand per year. Boulton and Watt maintained high prices for the use of their machine and blocked competitors from creating more efficient and cheaper machines, slowing down the potential progress of steam technology. By pursuing these legal cases, the pair established a dangerous precedent of using patent protection laws to suppress competition rather than using competition as a catalyst for improving their machine. Some historians estimate that because of their efforts, the progression of the Industrial Revolution was slowed down by at least one decade.

The steam engine was the first of many inventions that would completely change the economic and social structure of Britain in the 18th and 19th centuries. Once the patent expired in 1800, other steam engines came onto the market that could be adapted for use in even more industries, making things like textile production and mining more efficient and more lucrative for their owners. With that came new technologies that connected the world, like George Stephenson's steam locomotive, but it also brought with it a period of exploitation that restructured the country.

Chapter 3: Richard Arkwright's Water Frame

The late 1700s saw the rise of the factory system, which began with the textile industry before spreading into manufacturing and other industries. The factory system changed the structure of British working society and accelerated the progress of the Industrial Revolution. At the core of this shift was British inventor and industrialist Richard Arkwright, whose invention—the water frame—helped to increase productivity and efficiency within the textile industry and beyond.

Richard Arkwright: A Life of Innovation

Richard Arkwright was born on December 23rd, 1732, in Preston, Lancashire. He rose from humble beginnings to become one of the most well-known figures of the Industrial Revolution. He was the youngest of seven children, born to a tailor. Arkwright's family was too poor to send him to school, so they arranged for their youngest to be tutored by a cousin. Eventually, he was apprenticed to a barber.

Arkwright set up his own shop, and with the small income he received from his second marriage, he was able to expand his business and make innovations in wig making. Arkwright developed a method for dyeing hair that was more water-resistant than before; this was important at the time since wigs were expensive items that were easily damaged by rain or moisture, which could cause the wig to lose its shape or the dye to run. He also established an extensive network for collecting human hair to use in wig-making; Arkwright traveled throughout the countryside and connected with women who were willing to sell their hair to be used for wigs. These extensive travels often brought him into contact with women involved in weaving and spinning, so when the fashion for wigs started to decline in the mid-1700s, Arkwright turned his attention to textiles.

In about 1767, Arkwright met and began to collaborate with John Kay, a clockmaker from Warrington, a town just outside Liverpool. Arkwright recognized the potential of mechanizing the textile industry, and John Kay provided the technical expertise he needed to realize his ambition. John Kay had already been working with inventor Thomas Highs on a new spinning machine, but he was forced to abandon the project due to a lack of funds.

Working together in Preston, the pair developed what would later become the spinning frame, a machine that was capable of spinning 128 threads of fiber simultaneously. Arkwright and Kay worked in secret as they developed their prototype, and in 1769, Arkwright filed for a patent for the machine—one that did not acknowledge Thomas Highs's contributions to the invention. This omission led to a bitter falling-out. Nevertheless, the pair laid the foundation to transform manufacturing.

James Hargreaves and the Spinning Jenny

Before the water frame, textile production was a labor-intensive and time-consuming process that was primarily done at home. Spinning was not very efficient since it involved an individual spinner using hand- or foot-operated wheels that produced a single thread at a time. The process was also inconsistent in quality and not fit to meet the growing demand for textiles throughout the growing British Empire. Though spinning wheels were constantly evolving, it wasn't until the spinning jenny and water frame that the process was truly innovated. In 1764, James Hargreaves invented the spinning jenny, an invention that improved the efficiency of spinning but was still more catered to cottage industries. The spinning jenny allowed a spinner to operate multiple spindles at the same time (at first, it was 8, but eventually, the spinning jenny could spin up to 120 threads at a time).

A model of a spinning jenny.⁴

Hargreaves had worked as a hand loom weaver for most of his life, and he was inspired to invent the spinning jenny after seeing his wife's spinning wheel continue spinning after it had been overturned. At first, he built spinning jennies for himself and his neighbors, who were suspicious of what the machine might mean for the manual spinning industry. Hargreaves relocated to Nottingham, where he partnered with a man named Thomas James to establish a small mill so Hargreaves could continue working on his invention.

The spinning jenny consisted of a metal frame with 8 wooden spindles (up to 120 in later versions). A set of rovings (long, narrow bundles of fiber) was attached to a top beam on the frame, which passed through two horizontal wooden bars that could be clasped together and drawn out along the top of the frame to extend the spun thread. A spinner manually operated the machine by using their left hand to draw the bars along the top of the frame and using their right hand to quickly turn a wheel. The wheel caused the spindles to turn and spin the thread, which would be re-spun onto new spindles when the bars were drawn back to their starting position.

This machine became the first in a number of inventions that quickly changed the textile industry. It allowed one worker to produce multiple threads at once and dramatically reduced how much labor and time went into producing yarn. This invention also took spinning out of the home and into workshops, marking the first step toward the factory system of textile manufacturing. Hargreaves's machine and mill were fairly successful throughout his life, especially after some improvements were made later on, but the thread was still weaker and coarser than the thread crafted from traditional spinning wheels, limiting its commercial use.

Mechanics and Function of Arkwright's Water Frame

Arkwright's water frame addressed many of Hargreaves's inefficiencies. By using water power to drive the spindles, the machine was able to produce much stronger and more consistent yarn, and it was able to run continuously and could be scaled up in factories with multiple water frames installed side by side. The ability to have the machine run continuously (without a tired spinner at its helm) made it better for use in factories and helped to expand production. Its adoption led to the establishment of large-scale textile factories and revolutionized work and life in the Industrial Revolution.

The water frame consisted of four key components:
- Drafting Rollers: There were three pairs of rollers at the top of the machine that each rotated progressively faster than the last. The top rollers were covered with leather, while the bottom ones were fluted.
- Spindles and Flyers: Below the rollers were spindles equipped with flyers, which helped spin the yarn onto the bobbins. At first, the machine contained 8 spindles, but as improvements were made, the machine grew to have up to 120 spindles.
- Bobbins: These were below the spindles and were used to collect the spun yarn.

- Lifting Rail: This was a rail with plates that moved up and down. It evenly guided the spun yarn onto the rotating bobbins.

Prepared cotton was fed through the three pairs of drafting rollers at the top, first through the slowest. The rollers stretched and straightened the cotton fibers. The straightened fibers passed to the spindles and flyers below, where they were twisted together into a strand of yarn. The twisted (spun) yarn was then wound onto the rotating bobbins, as the lifting rail guided the yarn evenly onto the bobbin. The bobbins were removed and replaced with new ones once they were full, thus starting the process over again.

This process was not dissimilar to Hargreaves's spinning jenny, which employed the same basic principles. It also had rollers that fed fiber through a spindle and wound the spun thread onto bobbins. The spinning jenny was also powered by a wheel that allowed for multiple spindles to run at the same time. However, Arkwright's water frame had one key difference that allowed it to be more powerful and to run more consistently than the spinning jenny: water power. In each textile mill where the water frame was used, a large water wheel was installed to drive the spinning machines inside. Driven by the current of the river, the water wheel's rotary motion was transmitted to the machines inside the mill by a complex system of gears and belts. A main driving pulley drove a belt that turned the spindles, and two drums drove the drawing rollers at the top of the machine. This kept the two components in sync and created a more consistently spun thread. Another shaft that was closer to the ground operated the lifting rail.

Using water power allowed for continuous operation and significantly increased production capacity. No one was relying on a tired spinner to push a beam back and forth across the machine while also turning a spinning wheel. The fact that it relied on the water wheel also meant a person could install multiple machines in multi-story textile mills, each powered by a water wheel.

Patent Challenges and Protections

Arkwright filed the patent for the water frame in 1769, installing the first of many at his factory in Cromford in 1771. However, from the moment he filed the patent, he faced challenges from all sides. He fought with other manufacturers, a group known colloquially as the Lancashire Spinners, who were actively hostile to those holding exclusive patents. John Kay, who had patented the flying shuttle years prior, had to escape to France after finding himself in conflict with the same group of manufacturers. Arkwright also faced conflict from Thomas Highs, who maintained that he was the one to devise the concept of using rollers for spinning and that Arkwright merely financed the development and production of the water frame. Highs stated that Arkwright was not the inventor, nor had he come up with the original idea.

In 1781, this conflict intensified when Arkwright took legal action against nine spinning firms, which he claimed were using the water frame without a license. His legal case backfired. Rather than secure his rights to the water frame, it instead brought up, once again, the validity of Arkwright's patents. The manufacturers challenged Arkwright's exclusive patent on the basis that the originality of the idea and his participation in its development were questionable. A long court case followed, culminating in a patent trial in June 1785. As Arkwright attempted to extend the patent of the water frame and retain exclusive rights, a number of technicians testified that he had copied their original ideas, including Thomas Highs, the son of John Kay (John "French" Kay), and the widow of John Hargreaves, Elizabeth. They testified that Arkwright had stolen their original inventions or had used them as components in the water frame without acknowledging their origin.

As a result of the patent trial, the court rescinded Arkwright's patents in 1785, and his appeals were struck down. With his patents invalidated, Arkwright no longer had the exclusive right to use and license the water frame, which opened it up to widespread use. Other cotton manufacturers were free to use the inventions without restriction, leading to an explosive growth in cotton textile manufacturing, especially in Lancashire.

Despite the fact that he lost his patents, Arkwright had already amassed a considerable fortune and was hailed as a key figure of the textile revolution. There is no doubt that he was a skilled entrepreneur, and his creative use of the machine helped transform society at the dawn of the Industrial Revolution. For that, he was knighted by King George III in 1786. Arkwright died in 1792, leaving behind a substantial fortune and a transformative legacy.

The Factory System: A New Way of Working

The water frame was revolutionary not only for its ability to mass manufacture cotton yarn but also for how it restructured the way people worked and lived. It propelled the rise of factories, marking a massive turning point in the Industrial Revolution. We will explore the shift from the cottage industry to industrial production later on; for now, we will focus on the rise of the factory system and how Arkwright pioneered this new method of production at his cotton mill in Cromford, Derbyshire.

Cromford Mill

Arkwright established his cotton mill, Cromford Mill, in 1771. The mill was located close to the Derwent River so that it could use water to power the machinery inside. The layout of the mill was carefully designed to maximize the use of water power.

Arkwright installed an intricate waterworks system that ensured a consistent and powerful water supply, drawing from two main sources: the Cromford Sough, an underwater channel that collected wastewater from local lead mines, and the Bonsai Brook, a small tributary of the Derwent. Water was channeled through a series of aqueducts and tunnels that helped control the flow of water up to the machines in the mill. Later on, Cromford Mill created a small pond that provided water to new buildings as the factory continued to grow. Using multiple sources of water meant the mill could use multiple waterwheels to continuously generate power to the new machines—carding engines that prepared the raw cotton and pulled apart its fibers and the water frames that spun those fibers into cotton yarn.

The original mill was a five-story tall building. Another building was added in 1775, and the mill continued to grow, eventually comprising twenty buildings, including housing for the mill manager. In the 1840s, problems with the water supply forced the mill to cease its operations, and the buildings were repurposed throughout the years. They became a cheese warehouse, breweries, laundries, and even a dye house. Finally, in 1979, restoration efforts were taken on by the Arkwright Society. The mill now stands as a testament to this revolutionary moment in manufacturing and has been recognized internationally as a UNESCO World Heritage Site, along with other Derwent Valley mills.

Cromford Mill.⁵

Cromford Factory Towns

Arkwright's innovations and the success of the Cromford Mill had a profound effect on the way people lived and worked in 18th-century Britain. The factory system was a massive change from the traditional cottage industries and provided a new place of employment and a sense of independence for workers who might have been displaced by the enclosure system. When Cromford Mill was first built, it needed about two hundred workers to function at its highest capacity. However, there was no local infrastructure for all of these workers. There was no transportation to get them to the factory, and there was no place for them to live. To remedy this, Richard Arkwright built housing, a school, a chapel, a market, and even an inn to support his workforce in a new sort of community—the factory town. Factory towns were a new development that sprouted up across Britain, especially in the north, drawing people out of rural villages and into new industrial centers.

The development of factory towns and the new system of work introduced a life unlike anything experienced before. The flexible schedule of the cottage industry, in which most work was done at home, was gone. Instead, factory workers had to conform to the timetables set by the factory owners and the demand they had for production. Cromford, for example, had two shifts of twelve hours each, from 6 a.m. to 6 p.m. The gate to the mill was shut the moment a shift began, and those who didn't get through lost that day's pay and were fined to compensate for the loss of labor.

Most of the workers were women and children. Factory jobs allowed women, who were paid much less than their male counterparts, to get out of the home and work. Children were prized since they were able to get into small spaces to fix machinery that had clogged. The system shifted to prioritize unskilled workers who performed repetitive tasks. They were paid very little and faced poor conditions. Eventually, these conditions led to the formation of labor unions and workers' rights at the turn of the 19th century.

Chapter 4: The Transformation of the Textile Industry

Richard Arkwright's invention was not the last to transform the textile industry. After him came various innovators who took the slow, inefficient cottage textile industry and grew it into an enormous economic power for Britain.

The textile industry and its success expanded far beyond the shores of the United Kingdom, with implications felt all over the world. While we may think of the Industrial Revolution as being dominated by the steam locomotive and new communication networks, it was textiles that really drove the revolution at the beginning.

Pre-Industrial Textile Industry

At the beginning of the 18th century, Britain's largest industry and major export was textiles. They were produced mainly with British wool and then cotton and silk after the colonization of India. The entirety of textile production was done in the home in a decentralized system that prioritized skilled workers and individual producers. The process of creating cloth went through three distinct stages, which largely haven't changed even though the technology has: carding, spinning, and weaving.

The raw material (wool, for example) was first cleaned and carded, a process in which the raw fibers were brushed and combed to align the individual strands in preparation for spinning. Spinning took place at a manually powered wheel in the home, where a skilled worker, usually a woman, spun the carded fibers into thread. This was one of the most time-consuming aspects of textile production, and it was the first to be innovated with Hargreaves's spinning jenny. Hand spinning required years of experience and dexterity to create strong yarn that could be woven into cloth. The spun yarn was then passed on to a weaver, who operated a hand loom to interlace the warp and weft (the two basic components in weaving). The vertical warp yarns were held stationary in tension on a loom (frame) while the horizontal weft (also called the woof) was drawn through (inserted over and under) the warp thread. In the final stages, the textile workers would dye the cloth using vegetable-based dye before sending it off to market. The whole process was done at home, often from the collection of the wool to the dyeing process.

Cottage Industry and the "Putting-Out" System

The domestic way of working was referred to as the cottage industry or the putting-out system—a system where merchants acted as intermediaries between producers and markets. Merchants would also distribute raw materials to the producers. Workers maintained ownership of their tools and control over their schedules, and they worked as a family unit at home, with children or apprentices often inheriting the skills and tools. Merchants avoided the added cost of maintaining a workshop but still had access to a wide range of producers. Workers had an income alongside their domestic activities, which created a system with control on both sides of the coin, as well as a slow, seasonal production cycle.

Despite the fact that the putting-out system was significantly slower than post-industrialism systems, it kept people employed across the country. The export of woolen goods represented more than a quarter of all British exports for most of the 18th century. This system also created new production networks and pre-industrial regions that laid the foundation for industrialization later on. These production networks connected villages to the broader system, integrating them into international trade.

Social Structures

For rural, working-class families, the cottage industry created a unique pattern of work, social organization, and balance. Unlike the factory system, at-home textile production allowed families to balance manufacturing with agricultural demands (whether it was farming land, running a farm as a tenant, or having a domestic homestead).

Multiple family members contributed to the production process, with the tasks often divided along gender or age lines. The women were spinners, the men were weavers, and the children assisted with simpler tasks like cleaning and carding. Households functioned simultaneously as living and work spaces. Work happened according to the available daylight, the season, and fluctuating family needs rather than an externally imposed, rigid, twenty-four-hour schedule.

While the quality of life cannot compare to that of today, it generally gave the workers more flexibility than the factories that would replace it. Social life was also structured around this work, as spinning bees and similar communal activities combined productivity with socialization. Children learned from their elders through apprenticeships and family instruction, preserving skills across generations and ensuring that the older generation was taken care of. This created strong crafting communities with a strong cultural heritage.

However, the cottage industry system had inefficiencies that would lead to its eventual downfall once industrialization took hold. Production was restrained by how much could be produced by hand, and it proved difficult to meet the growing demand as the British Empire started to expand. Also, it was difficult to keep a quality standard of cloth or yarn since merchants purchased from various households, which created an inconsistent final product that could be difficult to sell. As factory owners used new mechanical machines to create a consistent product and managed hours to maximize efficiency, the putting-out system gradually became obsolete. Factory owners were able to increase production capacity and achieve mass production, which was impossible in domestic production, offering merchants and consumers more affordable goods. It also changed the nature of work and the lives of the working class.

Mechanization of the Spinning Process

The first step in industrializing the textile industry was the mechanization of the spinning process. Before Richard Arkwright set up his factories, other inventors created machines that offered more power to the manual spinning and weaving machines, dramatically increasing productivity for those working with textiles. This gradual build toward mechanization began with John Kay's invention of the flying shuttle in 1733. The flying shuttle allowed a single weaver to produce wider fabrics and work more quickly via a mechanical system that propelled the shuttle across the loom at high speeds, eliminating the need for weavers to manually pass the shuttle through the shed, in which the threads run vertically from the front of the loom to the back, and the weaver raises some threads while lowering others.

It used a smooth board called a race along the front of the loom to travel across wider looms. This innovation doubled production rates, reduced physical strain, and allowed a single operator to manage wider looms on their own. It also created a demand for faster fabric production, so, there was a need for faster spinning, carding, cleaning, and dyeing.

Despite the fact that John Kay was chased out of Britain by the crafter and merchant groups, other innovations quickly followed that changed the face of the textile industry. In the previous chapter, we learned about Richard Arkwright's water frame and James Hargreaves's spinning jenny—two inventions that ushered in the age of the factory system—but these inventions did not power the textile transformation alone. The spinning mule and the power loom were invented around the same time and contributed massively to this shift in textile production.

Samuel Crompton and the Spinning Mule

Samuel Crompton was born in Bolton, Lancashire, in 1753 to a family of smallholders (subsistence farmers) and weavers who had been working as crafters for generations. He learned the trade at a young age, spinning yarn alongside his mother at the age of five and working the loom by the time he was ten. His life was marked by hardship, as his father died when Crompton was young, leaving his mother to support their family through textile crafting and farming.

When he was fifteen years old, he began working on Hargreaves's spinning jenny but was frustrated by the weak and easily breakable yarn the jenny produced. With the goal of inventing a better spinning machine, Crompton began working in secret on a machine that combined elements of Hargreaves's spinning jenny and Arkwright's water frame, hiding his work from the local Luddites who opposed all mechanization of spinning. He financed his work with the earnings he made as a violinist in a local theater. After five years, he created a prototype for the hybrid: the spinning mule.

The only surviving example of the spinning mule built by Crompton.⁶

The spinning mule merged two key elements from the spinning jenny and the water frame. It enabled the simultaneous spinning of multiple threads of yarn, as with the jenny, and it used rollers to stretch and strengthen the fibers, like the water frame. Crompton's machine featured a moving carriage that went back and forth like the shuttle on a loom, with spindles that traveled up to 5 feet (1.5 meters) back and forth; slim rollers that evenly drew out the twisted fibers; a draw stroke that stretched and twisted the fibers into yarn; and a return stroke while the other carriage moved forward, winding the spun yarn onto bobbins. This whole process was powered by a single operator and could produce both warp and weft threads. The first mule Crompton made had eight spindles and could produce one pound of yarn per day, far surpassing manual methods and even other methods that had come to market.

Unfortunately, Crompton lacked the funding to secure a patent for his machine. It cost about £200, which would have been out of his means as a working-class inventor, and he had no investors to cover the cost. Crompton presented his machine at the Manchester Exchange, hoping to receive a payout for his invention, but the inventor only received £60, and his invention was then copied by factory owners throughout the north. Without patent protection, Crompton was not compensated, and he had no way to challenge their use, so he did not benefit from the spinning mule's popularity the way Richard Arkwright was able to with the water frame.

By 1812, at least 360 spinning mules were in use. Crompton attempted to receive compensation from Parliament. After a long, drawn-out battle that was hampered by the Napoleonic Wars and the death of a supportive prime minister, Crompton was awarded a mere £5,000 for his invention—barely a fraction of its worth. Even though he had revolutionized the textile industry, creating a booming economy for Britain and the factory owners, Crompton himself struggled financially until his death in 1827.

Edmund Cartwright and the Power Loom

Edmund Cartwright was a British clergyman and inventor. He was responsible for the machine that automated the final process in the textile factory—weaving. Cartwright was born into a wealthy family in Nottinghamshire, and as expected of his status, he was educated at Oxford. After leaving school, Cartwright dedicated himself to the Church of England, becoming ordained in 1767 and serving at Goadby Marwood in Leicestershire until 1786 when he became a prebendary in Lincoln Cathedral. He didn't have any particular connection to the textile or manufacturing industry, unlike many of the other inventors. It wasn't until he was forty-one and visited one of Richard Arkwright's factories that he decided to dedicate his life to inventing.

After observing Arkwright's water loom and mechanized spinning machines, Cartwright was inspired to create a similar machine that would automate the weaving process. His reasoning was that if spinning—a highly technical process requiring skill and human dexterity—could be automated, so could weaving. Between 1784 and 1785, Cartwright worked on his design. He received a patent for the first prototype in 1785. The power loom had five main components: the warp beam, the shuttle box, a reed, the shedding device, and a weft insertion mechanism. These were powered by either water or steam and worked together to automate the process of lifting and lowering warp threads while inserting weft threads between them. The worker only had to prepare and insert the warp and weft threads, with the machine automating the rest of the process. This dramatically increased the efficiency and speed of the weaving process.

The power loom wasn't a runaway success. In 1813, there were still fewer than three thousand power looms in operation throughout the country, in part because the initial invention was quite simplistic. Cartwright continuously improved his machine, and in the 1820s, it began to gain popularity, but this would come with a challenge. First, weavers were resistant to the machine, fearing that it would put them out of work. At one point, a Manchester factory with four hundred power looms burned to the ground in a probable arson attack by manual handloom weavers. Eventually, the power loom would become adopted more widely, but like Crompton's invention, Cartwright's machine was copied and adapted by factory owners who wanted to avoid paying for the patent. This, as well as a failed textile mill, eventually led Cartwright to appeal to the British Parliament for recognition of his contributions to the industry. This recognition came in 1809 when he was awarded £10,000—a significant sum that helped Cartwright get out of the debts he owed from his failed factory. He purchased a small farm in Kent, where he continued to invent and improve on his designs until his death in 1823.

These were only two of the many innovations that revolutionized the textile industry. The demands of textile manufacturing set off a chain reaction across Britain, as changes in transportation, trade, and even tooling began to cater to the needs of the mills. Steam locomotion and railways developed, as factory owners wanted a more direct and speedy connection between the coal mines that powered their factories and the ports that exported their product. Machine tool production became more advanced since all of these innovations required specialized tools for construction and maintenance, leading to new lathes, planers, and milling machines. In 1797, Henry Maudslay's screw-cutting lathe enabled tool makers to create standardized parts, which were perfect for factories that had many multiples of the same machine. These and many other developments created a ripple effect of invention out of the steam engine and the textile mill.

FIGURE 15. MAUDSLAY'S SCREW-CUTTING LATHE
ABOUT 1797

FIGURE 16. MAUDSLAY'S SCREW-CUTTING LATHE
ABOUT 1800

Maudslay's early screw-cutting lathes.[7]

The Textile Shift: From Domestic to Industrial Production

With the invention of the power loom and the spinning mule, all aspects of textile production could be automated and required significantly less skilled labor than ever before. Factory owners could purchase as many machines as could fit on a factory floor and pay little for the labor to run these machines day and night. This led to a rise in factories and a concentration of factory workers in industrialized towns. There was a huge shift from rural, domestic work that was governed by the needs of a household to industrial production driven by the profit from commerce.

Centralization of the Textile Industry

The water frame, spinning mule, and power loom all needed one thing to operate efficiently: water. Arkwright built his factory near a river to make use of the running water, and in later years, steam would take over as the major source of energy to power textile machines, which meant factories had to be close to sources of coal. Even if a spinner's or weaver's home was situated next to a river, the machines themselves were far too large (and expensive) to run at home, so factories began to replace homes as the main producers of textiles. Factories could consolidate all of the machines in one well-positioned location, managing everything from cleaning to dyeing fabric. When steam locomotives were introduced, they contributed to centralization by freeing factories from the need to be near a source of coal or water, instead tying them to transport hubs like Manchester, which was given the name "Cottonopolis" for its many cotton factories.

As factories became the norm and families were pushed out of communal lands, cities like Manchester saw explosive growth. Workers migrated to where they could find jobs in factories, which provided steady wages and work for both men and women. The work was year-round as well. Many of these factories were connected to "company towns," like Arkwright's Cromford Mill, which provided room, board, and (rarely) education for children.

However, factories often came with unsanitary and dangerous working conditions and poor wages. Children were sent to work when their parents needed additional income to supplement their low wages. Workers lived in overcrowded and unsanitary conditions, and they had little to no labor rights. If a worker suffered an accident and could not work, they had no protections to ensure they could recover. Wealth became concentrated among the few factory owners, who controlled the entire line of production and offered no flexibility to their workers. In fact, workers who missed a day due to illness were seen as unproductive. If they arrived late, they were punished either physically or by having their wages garnished. Oftentimes, they were required to pay back the cost of their lost labor to the factory owners, as well as the garnishment.

The centralization of factories became the basis for modern industrialist capitalism, which often prioritizes efficiency over craftsmanship. Industry could provide cheap, fast, and consistent materials and enhance economies, but it also solidified social inequalities, packing a powder keg for resistance movements and labor struggles.

Housing in London in the 1870s.[8]

The Luddite Movement

Those skilled workers who had built a solid livelihood through subsistence farming and textile making did not stand by as their work was replaced by faster machines. From the early days, many could see how mechanization would enable the exploitation of the working class, so they protested not against the actual machines but against what those machines could do to their lives. Named after the mythical figure Ned Ludd, a Robin-Hood-like character who destroyed a loom in a fit of rage, they targeted machinery like power looms and water frames, which they saw as a threat to their work. The Luddites were weavers, knitters, croppers, and everyone else who had seen their wages plummet thanks to factories and automation. And their protest did not end with the machines themselves. The Luddites also fought against the inflation from the Napoleonic Wars (which disproportionately affected the working class), food shortages, and the absence of protections for those who did work in the factories.

The movement began in Nottinghamshire in 1811, where knitters destroyed frames at a factory producing stockings. In a year, the protest had spread across Yorkshire, Lancashire, and the Midlands as Luddites destroyed steam-powered looms, mills, and threshing machines. They organized in secret, sending threatening letters signed by "General Ludd" before striking at the factories, all in order to avoid the equally violent retaliation of the government. The Frame-Breaking Act of 1812 made machine-breaking a capital offense punishable by hanging, and the British government deployed about twelve thousand troops to the north, where textile manufacturing was most popular, in order to suppress any open protests and hunt down Luddites meeting in secret. The government even employed informants who infiltrated these secret meetings and provided information on planned attacks.

In January 1813, a mass trial in York saw over sixty men charged with crimes related to Luddite activities; of those, seventeen were hanged for their crimes, and the rest were transported to penal colonies in Australia. These events were used as a public deterrent, sending a message that the Luddite movement would not be tolerant and that the government had chosen to align with the wealthy industrialists over workers' welfare.

Though the movement caused some destruction and short-term financial losses for factory owners, it could not stop the fast pace of industrialization, and the movement died out in about 1817. Some Luddites who had not been arrested, executed, or exiled shifted their attention to other labor movements like the Chartist Movement, which advocated for voting rights for working-class men.

Trade Expansion: New Networks, New Goods

By mechanizing textiles and creating the framework for mass production, the output of textiles from Britain increased dramatically, and manufacturers needed new markets for their goods. They were also able to produce new textiles much faster and more consistently than before. They no longer relied on a weaver's expertise with a particular type of fiber. This balance created a need and supply for new markets and new raw materials. Soon, a new network of commerce was born—one that crossed continents with the importation of raw fibers and the exportation of machine-made cloth.

The best example is the trade of Indian cotton and silk textiles. Trade in Indian cotton had already started to increase before industrialization, but the new factory systems helped to accelerate this trade. British manufacturers started importing huge quantities of raw cotton, which was spun in their factories day and night. At first, they mainly imported from India and the Caribbean, but after Eli Whitney invented the cotton gin in 1793, America was brought into the fold. By 1830, cotton accounted for 55 percent of British imports, highlighting just how quickly the textile industry had expanded and dominated the British economy.

This led to a fast shift in global power dynamics, as Britain's mechanical factories and cheap labor produced standardized and high-quality textiles more efficiently than traditional handcrafted goods from non-Western countries like India, displacing Indian producers and reversing centuries-old trading patterns. Rather than the British trading for elaborate silk and cotton cloth, they took the raw materials from Asia and exported their own mass-produced textiles. Protectionist policies like the Calico Act of 1770, which banned the import of most cotton cloth, further served to enhance British dominance in domestic manufacturing. Other textiles, like silk, went through a similar transition. The invention of the Jacquard loom in 1801 enabled the mass production of silk patterns and led to a similar reversal of trade lines. In this way, Britain became the world's center for manufactured textiles, importing raw materials from all parts of the empire and exporting the finished product.

The industrialization of textiles created a whole new global trade network, first in its new production scale, then with faster transportation and more economic interconnectedness. The textile revolution can be seen as changing an industry beyond its mechanics, as it resulted in a whole new system of international trade, establishing patterns of production, export, and consumption that we still see today.

The Textile Industry and the Slave Trade

It would be difficult to address the international trade of cotton during the Industrial Revolution without addressing the transatlantic slave trade. The new machines of the textile industry, in particular Eli Whitney's cotton gin, turned cotton processing from a slow and laborious task to an efficient operation. The cotton gin, combined with the spinning mule and power loom, made cotton production significantly more profitable and led to a boom in cotton production, which, in turn, increased the demand for slave labor.

British manufacturers needed raw cotton, and plantation owners in the Caribbean and the United States used enslaved labor to produce it since that made the process more profitable. In turn, African societies and colonies traded for textiles from India in exchange for captured individuals who would become enslaved on the plantations that produced the raw cotton. The textile industry was not the only one that encouraged the use of enslaved labor to cultivate and export raw goods; however, this example shows how the slave trade was a circle of profit and trade, one that mainly benefited European manufacturers and merchants.

Financial Evolution

By the early 19th century, traditional merchant banking was proving to be inadequate for the growing economy. The upfront capital needed for investing in new machinery and raw materials, combined with the complexities of global trade, surpassed the limits of the local banking system. In response to the growth of the textile industry, a new decentralized network of banking emerged in Britain. Country banks provided short-term credit to the regional manufacturers so they could acquire the capital needed to get their factories set up, while London banks acted as intermediaries, connecting these country banks with international trade markets. This new system created a financial hub in London and also helped to distribute risk and standardize currency across the different parts of Britain and the empire.

Soon, British finances evolved from a local credit system, in which a country bank determined credit based on assets and accepted the responsibility of the loan, to a national bill exchange network and cash-flow-based lending that took projected revenue into consideration when lending. This development established the foundation for modern corporate banking. Its emphasis on managing liquidity, balancing risk between country banks and London, and financing the whole supply chain is still reflected in global trade finance today.

Legacy of the Textile Revolution

The textile revolution transformed society, going far beyond the inventions of the power loom and the spinning mule. Out of textiles came the shift to mass production and factory work, new industries in machining and transportation, new forms of labor, urbanization—and all that barely scratches the surface of its influence! The textile industry revolutionized almost all aspects of private life and global connectedness, setting the foundation for the structure of modern society. Our current financial system, for example, reflects that same balance between local and global investment, and the system of trade and commerce can be traced back to the growth of cotton manufacturing and trade. The labor acts that provide many social protections for workers today are a result of protests that can be traced back to the start of the textile revolution. At the base of the Industrial Revolution lies the shift from domestic life to factory life, and this was all thanks to the innovations of the textile industry.

Chapter 5: Henry Bessemer and the Mass Production of Steel

By the mid-1800s, the Industrial Revolution was well on its way. Innovations in agriculture, manufacturing, and textiles helped the British Empire expand beyond Britain and Ireland, but there was still the problem of sustaining that expansion. While the ability to mass produce food and material goods had improved, the basic infrastructure of construction and transportation had not. Steel production, in particular, was still expensive, slow, and unreliable—until Henry Bessemer developed a new steelmaking process that created a stronger and cheaper material, one that could keep up with progress and withstand the test of time.

Henry Bessemer: Innovator of Steel

Henry Bessemer was born on January 19th, 1813, in Hertfordshire, England. He grew up to become a prolific inventor and engineer, but he wasn't the first Bessemer to do so! His father, Anthony Bessemer, was also an accomplished inventor and engineer. He had created a machine for the Paris Mint in France that could produce steel dies for creating medallions. He also became a member of the French Academy of Science in honor of his improvements to the optical microscope. Anthony Bessemer returned to England in the aftermath of the French Revolution and later would raise his son within this atmosphere of curiosity and invention, providing Henry Bessemer with his early exposure to engineering.

Henry Bessemer was mostly self-educated, thanks to his father's engineering workshop, and this alternative education allowed him to maintain an unconventional outlook and a willingness to challenge the status quo. His first major invention (when he was only seventeen years old) was a process for creating a fine brass powder that could be used to produce "gold" paint, which significantly reduced the cost of making the popular pigment. The profits from his early invention and the manufacture of this new brass "gold" paint allowed Henry Bessemer to have a small income, one that would give him the freedom to pursue other inventions, like a reusable embossing stamp for title deeds, a diamond polishing machine, and even a new method of creating graphite for pencils.

Experiments in the Crimean War

The invention that Bessemer would be known for came to him in the middle of the Crimean War, a conflict that lasted between 1853 and 1856 and was fought between the Russians and the Ottomans, British, and French for control of the Crimean Peninsula. At this time, the various militaries were still using cast iron cannonballs. Bessemer was motivated to develop a new projectile that was stronger and more accurate than the heavy cast iron balls. He developed a new artillery shell that rotated as it was fired, improving the ability to inflict damage and giving the cannonball better accuracy and a much higher range.

However, there was a major problem with his new invention. When Bessemer presented his new and improved cannonball to the French military, they told him that the force generated by this new artillery would break down the cast iron cannons, rendering them unusable after a single blast. Rather than give up, Bessemer focused his efforts on creating more durable cannons for military use, first by innovating the process for making cast iron.

Before Bessemer's inventions, cast and wrought iron were the more common materials used in construction and infrastructure; however, they both had significant limitations when it came to strength, durability, and cost. Cast iron was relatively cheap and could be used in large quantities, but it was weak and prone to cracks and breaks under stress; it was not the type of material one wanted for infrastructure projects. Wrought iron was also used in construction projects, and it offered more malleability than cast iron, but it wasn't strong enough to stand up to industrial use. At the time, steel was an expensive material. Producing steel was a time- and labor-intensive project, making it a material better used for small, luxury items like swords.

Bessemer began to experiment with metals to create a stronger cast iron, and in the process, he discovered a new process to manufacture steel. While experimenting with what would come to be known as the Bessemer process, he noticed that some pieces of pig iron (crude, high-carbon iron that had been smelted with coke and limestone) turned to steel shells without fully melting when exposed to hot air. Blowing hot air through the molten pig iron removed its impurities and carbon, resulting in malleable iron.

Bessemer realized there were three key aspects to creating malleable iron in this new process: speed, heat, and combustion. This insight formed the basis of the Bessemer process, which involved blowing air through molten pig iron to remove its impurities and adjust the carbon in order to create steel. Bessemer patented this method in 1855, along with the Bessemer converter—an egg-shaped furnace that facilitated the Bessemer process.

The Crimean War was almost at its end, but Bessemer's discovery became useful far beyond the battlefield.

The Bessemer Converter

The Bessemer converter was a revolutionary machine that was designed to facilitate the Bessemer process for converting pig iron into steel. The ovoid (egg-shaped) vessel stood at approximately 6 meters (19.7 feet) high and could convert about 30 tons of pig iron into steel in about 20 minutes. The converter required molten pig iron, air (for the oxidation process), and a refractory lining material to aid in combustion. This lining varied depending on the phosphorus content of the pig iron.

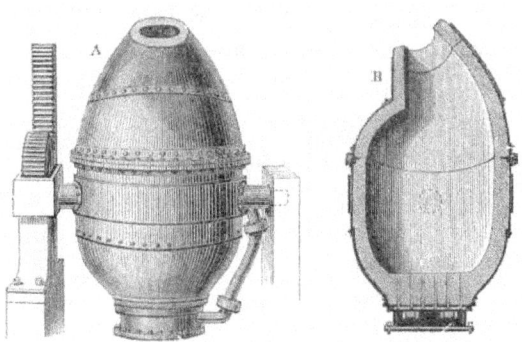

A diagram of the Bessemer converter.[9]

The key components of the Bessemer converter were:
1. Shape: The distinctive egg shape was designed to contain the violent combustion process within the converter. It had one offset opening at the top of the vessel, which was used to charge and pour the molten materials.
2. Lining: The interior of the converter was lined with a refractory material, usually dolomite, limestone, magnesite (for high-phosphorus iron), clay, or siliceous material (for low-phosphorus iron). The refractory lining allowed the converter to withstand the temperatures of combustion, and the material used facilitated the chemical reaction that removed the impurities from the type of iron being used.
3. Tuyeres: These were openings at the bottom of the converter where air was forced into the machine to start the oxidation process.
4. Pivoting Mechanism: A trunnion allowed the converter to be tilted. The machine was tilted backward at the beginning of the process to pour in the molten iron (charging). Then, it was turned upright during the process in order to contain the materials and combustion. It was turned forward at the end of the process to pour out the slag and molten steel (pouring).

This machine turned the process of making steel into a twenty-minute operation, making it possible to mass produce quality steel. At first, the converter was "charged," with molten pig iron poured into the vessel from its offset opening. Next, the converter was rotated upright, with the offset opened at the top to release any gases from the combustion process. Air was forced into the converter from the tuyeres at the bottom. This forced air started the oxidation process. It caused any impurities in the pig iron to oxidize, and they either escaped out of the vessel as gas or were separated at the top of the molten mixture as slag. The process could be monitored by observing the flame at the opening of the vessel until the "blow" was complete. Once the "blow" was over, carbon or other materials could be added to achieve the target steel properties. At the end, the finished steel was tilted out of the machine, and the slag was separated into waste.

Challenges with the Bessemer Process

Bessemer presented his process in 1856 in a paper titled "The Manufacture of Iron Without Fuel" to praise and widespread skepticism. Some recognized the ingenious potential of Bessemer's experiment, but many steelmakers were reluctant to adopt this process. They had already invested money and time into their own production and were reluctant to give that up for a method that was untested and required advanced technical knowledge. To fight against this, Bessemer offered the first few licenses at a low cost, encouraging steelmakers to take him up on it. Those who initially took on his license found inconsistent results. Sometimes, the process created metal that was brittle without any sort of fix or explanation for the failure. Bessemer was forced to buy back the licenses and continue experimenting.

Bessemer established his own steelworks in Sheffield, England, where he was able to continue his experiments, eventually concluding that it was high-phosphorus iron that was creating the inconsistent results. Around the same time, the Swedish government lifted its ban on exporting iron, which was naturally low in phosphorus, and he collaborated with Goran Grandson of Edsken Steelworks in Sweden, allowing Bessemer to make improvements to his design and import low-phosphorus iron for him to use at his own steelworks in Sheffield. He began to produce steel at a significantly lower cost than his competitors, underselling them by £15, which provided Bessemer with the means to continue experimenting.

His invention was not without legal challenges, though. William Kelly, an American inventor, had been working on a similar process and received a priority patent in 1857, which effectively nullified Bessemer's 1855 US patent and the licenses he held in the United States. In addition to that, another British engineer and inventor, Robert Mushet, claimed that it was his idea to add manganese as an additive to the process to help draw out the carbon—an addition that proved to be crucial to the Bessemer process's success. Mushet initially received no compensation for his work; it wasn't until later in his life, when Mushet was ill, that Bessemer agreed to give him an annual pension of £300, likely to keep him from pursuing legal action.

Basic vs Acid Bessemer Process

The original Bessemer process, as we have mentioned, was only consistent when it was done with low-phosphorus iron. In this process, the Bessemer converter was lined with clay, which did not absorb enough phosphorus to convert the high-phosphorus clay that was more common in Britain. Between 1875 and 1879, two cousins, Sidney and Percy Gilchrist, developed their improvement to the Bessemer process at the Blaenavon Ironworks in Wales. The cousins began their experiments in 1877, with Sidney traveling from London to Wales to work with his cousin Percy, who was employed as an analytical chemist at Blaenavon Ironworks. Their experiments began in secret, but eventually, the manager became aware of their work and provided them with a small Bessemer converter so they could conduct their tests.

Through experimentation, the cousins developed a new lining for the Bessemer converter that used dolomite or limestone. The stone could absorb the unwanted phosphorus and consistently create the steel product that was in demand. This modification became known as the "basic" Bessemer process, which was in contrast to the original "acid" process. This allowed steelworks to produce steel from either type of iron as long as they had a dedicated Bessemer converter with the correct lining.

Henry Bessemer revolutionized steelmaking, turning it into a cheap and easily mass-produced product as opposed to a luxury good. The process was imported to the United States by Andrew Carnegie, who became familiar with the Bessemer process in 1872 and incorporated it into his own steel empire. That being said, the popularity of the Bessemer process was short-lived, as by the 1890s, it was already being replaced by open-hearth steelmaking and Sir Carl Wilhelm Siemens's regenerative furnace. In the early years of the Bessemer process, steel output grew immensely, especially in the United States, paving the way for the modern steel industry and the rapid industrialization of the late 19th century and the Second Industrial Revolution.

Impact on Infrastructure and Machinery

The availability of cheap, high-quality steel had a significant impact on construction and infrastructure projects across the globe. The ratio of strength to weight and the durability of steel made it the ideal material for large-scale projects and as the skeleton of buildings and bridges, which were getting bigger and longer as trade expanded.

Railways experienced the most growth. Steel rails replaced iron ones since they lasted about ten times longer and could support heavier and longer locomotives, allowing for more goods to be transported over the same distance. Bridges also benefited from the popularity of affordable steel. Engineers were free to design longer bridges that were capable of supporting roads over wider rivers and deeper valleys. Iconic steel bridges, like the Brooklyn Bridge and the Forth Bridge in Scotland, were built in the late 19th and early 20th centuries. Steel was not only the skeleton; it was also other parts of bridges. A good example of this is the Vizcaya Bridge in Bilbao, a suspension bridge composed of iron beams and twisted steel ropes. These bridges, many of which still stand today, became icons of industrial progress, thanks to steel.

A view of the Forth Bridge being built in 1888.[10]

Also, in the early 20th century in particular, the popularity of steel enabled the construction of modern skyscrapers, forever changing city skylines and the ways people live. People were able to build taller, stronger buildings that could withstand the tests of time and efficiently use the limited space in major cities—a necessary evolution as factories and trade made urbanization more popular.

Between infrastructure and manufacturing was the renewed maritime industry, which underwent a major transformation with the introduction of affordable steel. Steel hulls replaced wooden ones, allowing for the construction of ships that were lighter, larger, and more durable—perfect for the burst of maritime trade that came along with the Industrial Revolution. These ships were able to withstand harsher conditions than the wooden-hulled ships of the past and carry much heavier loads. Long-distance sea travel was more feasible and safer for both traders and passengers. Passengers felt safe on cross-ocean voyages, and merchants felt secure that their cargo would arrive safely at its final destination.

Even the process of shipbuilding itself was revolutionized. Steel offered flexibility that wood wasn't capable of, as steel components could be welded together in new ways and remain watertight and sturdy. This new malleability allowed ships to be reshaped into new configurations and tailor-made designs. Shipbuilders could create small specialized vessels, massive cargo ships, or passenger cruisers.

Woven through all of these infrastructure elements was the machinery that made the impressive feats of the Industrial Revolution possible. Once again, factories and manufacturing were revolutionized thanks to the availability of cheap, high-quality steel. Steel machinery was stronger, more precise, and more durable than its cast iron predecessors, leading to the development of better machines. In the textile industry, steel components added to existing machines, like the power loom, made them lighter and more energy efficient, allowing for even faster production times.

Experiments in Metallurgy

Henry Bessemer's experiments had a snowball effect in experiments in metallurgy. Scientists and engineers were fascinated by his process and began to experiment further, not only in regard to how steel can improve existing machinery but also with the study of metallurgy itself (the study of metal properties and their production and purification). The Bessemer process was the first to quickly and cheaply create steel from pig iron, but it was soon surpassed by other processes. The open-hearth process (also known as the Siemens-Martin process) was developed very shortly after the Bessemer process became popular. It offered better control over the final chemistry of the steel. It could produce larger quantities of steel and use more scrap metal, making the process more versatile, although it was slower than Bessemer's converter. The steel process continued to be refined into the 20th century when basic oxygen steelmaking emerged as an improvement upon both methods.

Chapter 6: George Stephenson and the Steam Locomotive

When thinking about the Industrial Revolution, most will automatically think of a steam train, blazing new trails. The textile, agricultural, and manufacturing revolution preceded it, and it could never have happened without the advent of steel. However, the changes that came with railways were so massive that railroads became the stock image for the Industrial Revolution.

Few figures loom as large as George Stephenson, the engineer and inventor whose work building the steam locomotive earned him the title "Father of Railways." Born into a poor family, Stephenson rose through the ranks and followed his curiosity, culminating in the construction of the Stockton and Darlington Railway, the first public railway to use steam locomotives.

Like the many inventions that came before, the steam locomotive revolutionized life beyond its industry. New railways facilitated urbanization, accelerated industrial growth and productivity, and connected distant regions in a way that had never been seen before. Travel was suddenly significantly cheaper, and goods could go farther, opening up new markets for merchants and consumers.

George Stephenson: A Brief Biography

George Stephenson was born on June 9th, 1781, in Northumberland, where the Industrial Revolution was already transforming the livelihoods of those who lived there. His parents were poor. His father worked for a low wage as the fireman of a colliery (coal mine) in Wylam. Incidentally, his father also operated a Newcomen atmospheric engine, which we learned about previously. Stephenson's parents were both illiterate and unable to afford an education, as was the case for many working-class laborers at the time.

Like many children, George was expected to start working as soon as he was able in order to supplement the low wages of his parents. He started working at the age of eight, herding cows to prevent them from straying into the wagonways, the early form of horse-drawn railway that transported coal from the mines. A few short years later, he joined his father at the Waylay Colliery as a picker, sorting stones and debris from coal in the pithead. Eventually, George worked his way up to become an engine man and then a brakeman at the same colliery. In his late teens, George became curious about news of the Napoleonic Wars happening on the European continent, which inspired him to work toward an education. At the age of eighteen, he took classes at night in literacy and arithmetic. He continued this commitment to education later when he was a father, prioritizing his son's education and studying alongside him.

Early Career Success: Stephenson the Engineman

George Stephenson's professional life began in earnest when he started as an engineman at Water Row Pit in Newburn, where he operated a lift that hauled coal up from the mines. In 1801, he advanced to become the brakeman at Black Callerton Colliery, managing the same machine—a role that required precision and accuracy and brought him up close to the machinery used in the coal mine. During this early period, Stephenson worked for various collieries in the north of England and in Scotland. He was known to take machines apart and clean them, learning how they worked in the process. He also learned how to make and mend shoes and clocks in order to make a little extra money on the side. Despite personal tragedies (his wife, Frances, and their infant daughter both died of disease in 1806), Stephenson's reputation grew as a competent machinist and budding engineer as he settled in West Moor at Killingworth Colliery.

Stephenson's first big breakthrough happened at Killingworth when he managed to resolve a critical malfunction in the main pumping engine of the colliery, the success of which earned him a promotion to enginewright. In modern terms, it would be the equivalent of a chief mechanic in a similar facility. The new position granted him a little more autonomy and the opportunity to travel to other collieries to see the types of machines and engineering they used. In 1813, Stephenson visited a neighboring colliery to observe John Blenkinsop's new locomotive: a steam boiler on wheels that was being used to haul coal out of the mines. Believing he could improve upon the machine, Stephenson petitioned the owner of Killingworth, Thomas Henry Liddell, 1st Baron Ravensworth, to allow him time and funds to create his own locomotive.

The *Blücher* and Safety Lamp

In 1814, Stephenson debuted the *Blücher*, a steam-powered locomotive that could pull a train of eight loaded wagons carrying thirty tons of coal at four miles per hour. At the time, the price of corn was at an all-time high due to the Napoleonic Wars, and Stephenson used the opportunity to try to find a way to replace the horses that typically pulled the coal trains, saving money for Killingworth. The *Blücher* consisted of a cylindrical wrought iron boiler. Inside the boiler was a single flue tube, about twenty inches in diameter, which acted as the main conduit. Water in the boiler was heated to produce steam at a pressure of about fifty psi (pounds per square inch). The engine was made up of two vertical cylinders, each with an eight-inch bore and a twenty-four-inch stroke that were immersed in the boiler, which helped to keep the cylinders warm. The pressurized steam from the boiler was admitted into each end of the cylinders, driving the pistons up and down. The pistons were connected to a crankshaft, which was geared to wheels mounted on smooth iron rails.

The design incorporated several features that Stephenson had already observed and thought to improve upon, including the multi-tube boiler and a separate firebox (similar to Newcomen and James Watt's steam engines) and the use of iron rather than wood rails to keep the wagons running smoothly. Despite all of this, Stephenson wasn't satisfied. He would continue to work on the locomotive, creating new versions, including the *Rocket,* which won the Rainhill trials in 1829.

This wasn't the only invention he would work on while at Killingworth. In 1815, Stephenson began to develop a safety lamp that could burn in the coal mines without the risk of explosion. Unbeknownst to him, a prominent scientist named Humphry Davy was also developing a safety lamp for use in mines, one whose design was similar to Stephenson's. The pair both presented their designs to the Royal Society for patent consideration, but only Davy received the £2,000 prize. The situation created a lot of resentment on Stephenson's part, as he was aware that his Northumberland working-class accent created the image that he was an unscientific man and could only have stolen the design from Davy. The local community rallied around Stephenson and awarded him £1,000. It wasn't until 1833 that Stephenson would get proper recognition for his lamp, though it would be widely used in the northeast of England. It was known as the Geordie lamp. Stephenson's lamp was a glass cylinder encased with a perforated plate, allowing air to flow into the lamp and charge the flame while protecting it from coming into contact with the dangerous gases and firedamp (flammable gas) down in the coal mines.

Stephenson's years at Killingworth laid the groundwork for his later achievements, including the Stockton and Darlington Railway. These early locomotives were designed for hauling coal, but they introduced principles like the steam-blast exhaust system, which increased the boiler's efficiency by redirecting extra steam into the chimney. Unlike many other scientists and inventors of his time, Stephenson's inventions came from hands-on problem-solving in the coal mines.

The Steam Locomotive

Along with James Watt's improved steam engine came the idea for a steam-powered locomotive. The earliest steam carriage was designed by Nicolas-Joseph Cugnot in 1769. It was a three-wheeled machine used for hauling artillery, but it could only reach a top speed of about three kilometers an hour (two miles per hour). For a modern comparison, Cugnot's steam carriage had a top speed that is about the same as a robot vacuum or a parade float. In 1804, Richard Trevithick introduced the first steam-powered locomotive, successfully hauling a train (still made up of carriages with wooden wheels) along the Pen-y-darren ironworks tramway in South Wales. This was the first viable steam-powered "train," although the train was too heavy for the unstable track. In 1811, John Blenkinsop sought to fix the track problem by introducing a rack-and-pinion design: a rail that consisted of a cog wheel attached to the side of a locomotive that ran on a toothed rail. This design provided more stability and a little bit of propulsion for the locomotive.

In 1813, William Hedley and Timothy Hackworth, two engineers at Wylam Colliery, designed an improved locomotive called the *Puffing Billy*. It was the first locomotive built specifically to replace horses on the tramways at Wylam. This design inspired Stephenson to build the *Blücher*, and it became the blueprint for other steam locomotives across the north of England.

Locomotion 1 and the Stockton and Darlington Railway

With the network of factories and mines in the north, a modern railway system was becoming more and more important as the Industrial Revolution went on. The Stockton and Darlington Railway would connect the collieries of West Durham to the port of Stockton, reducing transport costs and time. It would also serve as a passenger railway once the network of collieries became more connected. The Stockton and Darlington Railway Company was established in 1821 by a group of businessmen who owned collieries in the north, and George Stephenson made sure he was a part of it. In part thanks to his work at Killingworth and the success of the *Blücher*, he was named as the Stockton and Darlington Railway's chief engineer in 1822. He persuaded the group to prioritize steam engines over horses for this new, modern railway.

The Stockton and Darlington Railway opened on September 27th, 1825. Its first haul, powered by Stephenson's *Locomotion No. 1*, was an eighty-ton load of coal and flour taken over a distance of nine miles at about fifteen kilometers per hour. The *Locomotion* also had one passenger car, "Experiment," promoting the ability of the train to carry people as well as materials. At its helm was George Stephenson, along with his son Robert, solidifying his reputation as the pioneer of steam locomotion and travel.

The Stockton and Darlington Railway proved to be a massive success, saving a significant amount of money and time for the factory owners in Manchester and Lancashire. Interestingly, the first "train," *Locomotion No. 1*, did not have brakes on its engine; instead, the brakes were fitted to the carriages behind it.

Standard Gauge

Working with locomotives was not Stephenson's only responsibility as chief engineer. This job required careful planning of the railroad's routes and expansion, including building railways that were steady and caused the least amount of friction while transitioning from horse-drawn wagonways. He settled on a gauge of four feet, eight inches, in part because he was already familiar with that gauge—it was the same gauge used on other mine car tramways. In doing so, Stephenson made it easier for mine carts to travel on these new railways. They did not have to be rebuilt or refitted; they could easily be attached to a locomotive with connections to the tramways.

He adjusted this measurement only once. In 1830, while building the Liverpool and Manchester Railway, he increased the gauge by half an inch in order to reduce friction between the wheel flanges and the rails. Over time, this became the standard gauge for rail tracks. Part of this standardization was because Stephenson and his son, Robert, who began working with him in 1821, were so successful that Stephenson began to design railways all across England. Eventually, British Parliament mandated that the gauges be four feet, eight and a half inches throughout the rest of England in order to maintain uniformity in its locomotives.

When train travel was introduced in North America, many expected to be using British locomotives, so they built to the British standard. Having different gauges, especially broader gauges, meant changing vehicles, leading to too much variety in equipment. While at first, like in England, some railways were built to different gauges, the American Civil War demonstrated the difficulty and inefficiencies of not having a standard gauge. Eventually, the American and Canadian railways also conformed to the British standard gauge.

While this was not a deliberate move on Stephenson's part, it is notable that the distance he chose was in line with road vehicles from ancient Roman times. Ultimately, the standard gauge came about due to practicality and popularity. Had Stephenson preferred a broader gauge, we could have been looking at a completely different standard today. However, it is interesting to consider that this distance had been around long before industrialization made it the "standard."

Rocket and the Liverpool and Manchester Railway

With the success of the Stockton and Darlington Railway, George Stephenson and his son moved on to their next major project: the Liverpool and Manchester Railway. The L&MR opened on September 15th, 1830, and was the next major milestone in steam locomotion and the growth of the railway. Unlike the S&DR (Stockton and Darlington Railway), the Liverpool and Manchester Railway was designed from the start for passenger transport. It was the first to have regular passenger service between the two major cities (Liverpool and Manchester), with a timetabled service and a signaling system for the trains. As with the Stockton line before, it also facilitated an easy way for manufactured goods from Manchester to reach the port city of Liverpool.

The opening of the Liverpool and Manchester Railway.[11]

The railway was a major success. By connecting two major cities (rather than a network of rails connected to collieries and factories), opportunities for work and travel opened up between them. It also ushered in a new age of communication, with faster transport of newspapers and mail between the cities and to the stops in between. With the introduction of the train signaling system and by having two parallel tracks, transport times improved, setting new standards for rail construction.

Its engineering improvements didn't stop there. Because of the landscape between Liverpool and Manchester, the L&MR introduced tunnelling and rock cutting to railway construction, once again innovating how these tracks were planned and laid. Once it opened, the railway was a massive financial success, paying its investors an average dividend of 9.5 percent over its fifteen years of existence. It kicked off a trend of railway speculation and expansion that came to be known as "Railway Mania," which lasted between 1830 and 1845.

Specially designed for this railway was Robert Stephenson & Company Limited's newest machine: *Rocket*. Despite only being founded in 1823, the company certainly hit the ground running. In 1829, the company behind the Liverpool and Manchester Railway announced a competition to find the best locomotive for its new line. The competition was dubbed the Rainhill trials. Stephenson's *Rocket* vastly outperformed all the other entries, reaching a top speed of fifty-nine km/h (thirty-six mph), cementing Stephenson's reputation and setting the design standard for steam trains for the next ten years.

The *Rocket* was an improvement upon *Locomotion No. 1* in that it had a more sophisticated steam engine and utilized the steam blast for better propulsion and to haul heavier cargo. It was perfect for a railway that was meant to carry passenger carriages as well as cargo. The *Rocket* had a mule-tubular boiler with twenty-five copper firing tubes, improving heat transfer throughout the engine, and a new wheel arrangement that made the locomotive lighter and smaller. The *Rocket* had a 0-2-2 wheel arrangement, meaning it had no leading wheel (unpowered wheels at the front of the train), and the driving wheels were located directly below the cylinders, allowing for the faster transfer of power from the pistons to the wheels. This created a more balanced and stable locomotive while also reducing its weight. This meant the engine could carry more cargo since it wasn't working so hard to power the driving locomotive. The *Rocket* was awarded first prize at the Rainhill trials and was used by the Liverpool and Manchester Railway on its opening day.

Rocket, which is preserved in the Science Museum in London.[12]

Transformation of the Railways

The Liverpool and Manchester Railway set off a fifteen-year period of rapid railway expansion across England, which spilled over into Continental Europe and North America. Railway Mania created a dangerous economic bubble, as speculation and investment in railways grew to an all-time high. The consequences of this growth spread into other parts of the British economy, including industrial growth and trade. The expansion also led to a period of drastic social transformation, spurring urbanization and social mobility.

Changing Industries, Shifting Markets

As more railways were planned and built, the demand for iron (and later steel) to build tracks, locomotives, and carriages breathed new life into these industries. British iron production, for example, increased by nearly 2,500 percent from 1796 to 1854, largely thanks to railway construction. This industrial boom created new jobs, shifting the economy further away from agriculture and textiles and more toward manufacturing and transportation. The north of England, which had traditionally been less economically prosperous than the south, began to grow, as more factories, collieries, and other industries set up shop there, thanks to the extensive railway networks in the region.

Beyond manufacturing, railways opened up previously inaccessible markets, boosting trade and commerce in other industries. Mining, metalworking, and even fishing flourished with improved transportation. The speed of locomotives meant it was easier to transport food and keep it fresh, revolutionizing nutrition and giving people better access to good food no matter where they lived.

Railways and Accessibility

With access to the railway networks, in particular the Stockton and Darlington Railway and the Liverpool and Manchester Railway, businesses were able to set up factories outside of urban centers while still having an efficient method of transporting their product. This led to the growth of new industrial towns and suburban areas, as more people were able to commute by train and live farther away from the places they worked.

For the first time, people weren't tied to their work or the city where they were born, leading to shifting demographics and a change in traditional social structures. Passenger railways made travel, like weekend vacations and day trips, accessible to more people. With carriages, laborers (who could afford it) had to take days off work in order to make trips to the seaside or visit distant family. With the steam locomotive, the same trip could be made in a few short hours. For example, by 1850, a train journey between London and Edinburgh took less than twelve hours; by carriage, it took two days. The introduction of a mail train made communication and the flow of information faster all across Britain, giving more people access to news and education.

Railway travel and steam locomotives left a mark beyond Britain. It transformed North America, opening up the West in a way that wasn't possible before. The extensive railway network built during Railway Mania formed the backbone of Britain's transportation infrastructure, and a lot of it is still in use today.

Steam locomotives continued to be developed, evolving into new forms. The diesel locomotive opened the door to electric vehicles, with new lightweight materials and aerodynamic designs. Today, heritage railways and museums house many of the original locomotives that were in use in the mid-1800s and are a major tourist attraction throughout the United Kingdom.

George Stephenson's contributions to Britain's railways continued for years. He continued working with his son, and in 1847, he became the first president of the Institution of Mechanical Engineers. His impact cannot be overstated. His ideas set the foundation for timekeeping, signaling, and logistics that had a reach far beyond railways.

Chapter 7: Samuel Morse and the Telegraph

The world was becoming more connected than ever before. Railways and steel made travel cheaper and faster, but there was one final piece of the puzzle to truly create a connected, globalized world. The telegraph, invented in the late 18th century, made communication easier across great distances. Why wait for a letter, which could take days, when you could send a message over an electric signal and have it arrive instantly? This new technology enabled the world to receive news in an instant, something we take for granted today. One's relatives, global affairs, and news events were suddenly available almost as soon as they happened, thanks to a new technology and alphabet developed by Samuel Morse.

Samuel Morse Biography

Samuel Finley Breese Morse was born on April 17th, 1791, in Charlestown, Massachusetts. He began his career as an artist, but a tragedy would make him change focus and dedicate his life to invention and electrical engineering. As a young man, his father wanted him to follow in his footsteps and pursue a career as a pastor. So, he sent Morse to Yale College for a formal education. It was there that Morse began to balance his studies in religious philosophy and science with a growing passion for painting. He learned about electromagnetism and was a member of the Society of Brothers in Unity—a literary and debating society at Yale. But throughout all this, Morse continued to pursue painting, and after his graduation, he apprenticed with Washington Allston in London.

As a painter, he studied the Renaissance masters at the Royal Academy. Many of his paintings from this period demonstrate his commitment to mythical themes and dramatic compositions, like *Dying Hercules* (1812). Upon returning to the US, Morse was forced to shift his attention away from the large-scale painting that was popular in Europe to portraiture in order to earn an income. His Eurocentric style didn't translate, and the strong problem-solving instinct that had been drilled into him at the Royal Academy kicked in. He became a prominent portrait artist, painting famous figures like American President James Monroe. He also founded the National Academy of Design.

In 1825, Morse's life would change in an unexpected way, turning him away from painting and toward his curiosity about electromagnetism. In February of that year, Morse was given a commission by the city of New York to paint Marquis de Lafayette, the hero of the American Revolution, during his visit to Washington, DC. The trip started with a great deal of hope. His wife, Lucretia, wrote to him expressing her encouragement and pride at the commission despite the fact that she was eager to have her husband back at their home in Connecticut, then a four-day journey away from Washington.

Morse replied, hoping to hear from his wife again, but instead, he received a devastating letter. Rather than another page of encouragement and love, Samuel Morse received a letter from his father stating that Lucretia had died during childbirth. The letter had taken four days to arrive. Even though Samuel set off back to New Haven immediately, he still arrived two days after his wife was buried. His last letter to her was dated February 9th, 1825—two days after the day she died. From that day forward, Samuel Morse dedicated his life to finding a new, faster method of communicating across long distances. He continued painting, but alongside that, he began to learn more about new technologies and electricity.

Development of the Telegraph

Samuel Morse continued his painting career, but he had a new focus. He was no longer dedicated to finding a way for his Eurocentric style to fit in with American painting; now more than ever, his painting career was a means for something else. His decision to transition to a new career drew criticism from his peers, who saw painting as an elite art and technical engineering as a lowly profession.

The transition also required Morse to retrain and become familiar with a new industry. Until then, he only had an education in art and religious philosophy, so finding funding for his new experiments proved difficult since he had no technological basis to draw from or help prove his worth to investors.

His shift from painting to invention began in earnest in 1832 during a transatlantic voyage from France back to the United States. Morse had been in France painting *Gallery of the Louvre*, and on the trip back, he encountered Charles Thomas Jackson, an American geologist, who demonstrated some principles of electromagnetism. Morse had already met him in his debate society at Yale and while he was studying in Britain, but this trip inspired him to take scientific practice more seriously. Upon returning to the US, Morse worked on a single-wire telegraph system to transmit coded messages. By using the problem-solving and material experimentation that had been encouraged at the Royal Academy, he found a way to repurpose a canvas stretcher to be used as a receiver frame for the machine.

Gallery of the Louvre by Samuel Morse.[18]

Collaboration with Alfred Vail

In 1835, Morse took up a position at New York University as a professor of fine arts. The position offered no pay, but the college did provide a small workspace on campus where Morse was able to establish a small studio and a laboratory. Morse continued painting, but he also began experimenting with the capabilities of electromagnetism and communication. He began to visit the college's mineralogical workshops, which were overseen by the chemist Leonard Gale. He became a close friend to Morse and provided many critical insights into electromagnetism, providing the scientific education that Morse lacked. By 1837, Morse had developed a pendulum-based register that could transmit coded signals, but the machine was still unreliable and limited in what it could transmit.

Nevertheless, Morse started demonstrating his machine in lectures at NYU, hoping to attract investors to the project. It was at one of these lectures that Alfred Vail, a young NYU alum, was introduced to him. Vail was trained as a machinist at his family's factory, Speedwell Ironworks, and immediately recognized the potential for the machine. He persuaded his father to invest $2,000 and provide a workspace at the ironworks where Vail could help Morse perfect the machine.

The pair were perfectly complementary to one another. Morse understood the theoretical principles of electromagnetism, while Vail had the mechanical experience to turn that theory into practical application. The two signed a contract, along with Vail's father, that stipulated they would work together to create a prototype by January of 1838. Vail and his assistant, William Baker, worked to create a reliable working prototype, with Morse keeping track of their progress from New York, mostly by mail.

On January 6th, 1838, the telegraph machine was finally ready for its first demonstration. The machine was limited by a distance of about 2 miles (3.2 kilometers), so for the demonstration, the pair wound 2 miles of wire inside one of the factory houses of Speedwell. Vail's father set down a message for his son to send, which Alfred Vail wrote out on the machine in code (a rudimentary system where each letter of the alphabet was assigned a word in the dictionary). At the end of the wire, Samuel Morse transcribed what was written as it was churned out: "A patient waiter is no loser."

Vail, his assistant, and other machinists at Speedwell made improvements to the machine and to telegraph communication in general. They replaced the pendulum with a spring-loaded arm and steel stylus that inscribed dots and dashes on paper tape, which created a faster and more reliable machine than Morse had built. Vail also co-created Morse code, a system of dots and dashes that correspond to various letters in the alphabet. Vail assigned the shortest sequences with the letters that appeared most frequently in the English language, making the code more efficient.

Mechanics of the Morse-Vail Telegraph

The Morse-Vail telegraph would continue to be improved over the years, but the basic concept remained the same. The telegraph consisted of a few key components:

- Battery: A battery provides the electrical current to operate the machine.
- Key: A single "key" acts as a switch, controlling the flow of electricity through the machine.
- Electromagnet: Located on the receiver, the electromagnet converts the electrical signals into mechanical movement.
- Register: This is a pen (Morse initially used a pencil, but Vail updated this to a steel pen nib) that recorded the oncoming signals onto paper tape.
- Cable: This is the long wire that connects the sending and receiving stations.
- Ground Connection: The circuit uses the Earth as a return conductor, so it needs to be connected to the ground.

When the operator pressed the telegraph key, it completed an electrical circuit, sending a current from the battery through the wire to the receiving station. At the receiver, the electromagnet was energized and attracted the register (Vail's steel armature). This movement produced an audible click by striking a metal rod, so the receiving operator could "hear" the message. It marked the paper tape, creating a "written" record of the transmission. The messages were encoded using Morse code. A long press created a dash, and a short press created a dot. Each was standardized for a specific length of time, and there was an alphabet that senders and receivers would memorize so they could send messages quickly across the line.

The genius of this system lay in its simplicity. In contrast to the multi-wire system of Cooke and Wheatstone, the Morse telegraph was easier and cheaper to install and maintain. Morse code was easily translatable to other languages since the dots and dashes corresponded to letters rather than specific (English) words.

The First Telegraph

Samuel Morse spent the next year doing presentations and attempting to get more funding for the machine. He traveled to Washington, seeking federal sponsorship, but he was rejected. He traveled back to Europe. Once there, he found that the Cooke and Wheatstone telegraph, a six-wire telegraph, had already taken priority in terms of funding and popularity throughout the British Empire. The first public demonstration of his machine wasn't until 1844. So, what was Samuel Morse doing in the time between?

Morse faced years of skepticism, legal disputes, and rejection before he completed his famous demonstration in Washington in 1844. His trip to Europe was unsuccessful (though he did return with a daguerreotype machine, which was one of the earliest cameras available, and taught others to use it in New York), and the creators of the Cooke and Wheatstone telegraph (who acquired their patent in 1837) accused Morse of copying their design. This meant that while gathering the extensive documents to file his own patent, Morse was also battling to prove that he had created his design independently and that it predated Cooke and Wheatstone's machine. Another inventor, Carl August von Steinheil in Germany, also registered a dispute, arguing that he was working on a single-wire telegraph at the same time as Morse. If that wasn't enough, Morse was also battling critics of his invention who dismissed it as nothing more than a toy or piece of science fiction. These battles drained what little funding Morse could secure for his invention, delaying his ability to commercialize and promote his machine. Finally, in 1840, he was granted a patent by the United States.

In December 1842, while still struggling to fund his machine amidst patent challenges and widespread skepticism, Morse made a trip to Washington, DC, to demonstrate his telegraph system to members of Congress. He strung wires between two committee rooms in the Capitol Building and, like he had done in the Speedwell Ironworks, sent messages back and forth between the two rooms, showcasing the immense potential of his invention. Congress was so impressed that it granted $30,000 (the same value as about $1.1 million today) for the construction of a telegraph line between Washington, DC, and Baltimore, Maryland, along the Baltimore and Ohio Railroad.

In May of that same year, the line was ready for its first demonstration. On May 24th, 1844, Samuel Morse transmitted the first message across a telegraph from the Old Supreme Court Chamber in the basement of the United States Capitol Building to Alfred Vail at the Mount Clare Station in Baltimore.

"WHAT HATH GOD WROUGHT"

The phrase was taken from the Book of Numbers in the Bible. It was recommended to him by Annie Ellsworth, the daughter of one of his supporters. The phrase evoked the excitement and awe that Morse wanted people to feel about this new technology, and it would continue to be used when people reflected on the power of new inventions.

This transmission became a major milestone in the Industrial Revolution. Information could be sent almost instantly over long distances, far surpassing the speed of traditional methods. The manufacturing, agricultural, and transportation industries had all advanced, and finally, communication was beginning to catch up.

The Expansion: Telegraphs Across America

After the success of the first transmission, telegraph lines quickly spread across the country. By 1846, a commercial line between New York and Boston had been completed, allowing for faster transmission of news from Europe. Only four years later, approximately twelve thousand miles of telegraph lines from twenty different companies had been built in the United States. At the end of the century, the whole country would be connected by telegraph wires, allowing for fast communication between the farthest parts of the continent, including Canada.

The 1850s saw huge growth in the spread of telegraph lines, reaching Southern states like Virginia and North Carolina and extending to Texas, thanks to the Valley Printing Telegraph Company, which later became known as Western Union. The telegraph's impact extended beyond personal communication too. During the American Civil War, it proved to be invaluable for tactical, operational, and strategic communications, contributing to the Union's victory. The US Military Telegraph Corps laid approximately fifteen thousand miles of line by the war's end, which were repurposed for public communication after the Civil War ended.

The growing telegraph network did not isolate itself to the United States either. In the 1850s, submarine cables began to lay down telegraph connections across oceans, the first of which crossed the Cabot Strait from Nova Scotia to Newfoundland in Canada. This was intended to be the first in a planned transatlantic line that would connect New York to London. Families that had been separated by the Atlantic could now communicate faster, providing a greater social network and personal connection to their distant relatives.

Societal Impact

The expansion of the telegraph had a profound influence on all aspects of American society. It accelerated westward expansion and stimulated economic growth, especially in the growing finance and commerce industries. One effect that has often been overlooked is the telegraph's role in standardizing time across the US. Before, local communities would maintain their own time standards based on the position of the sun, and this governed their day-to-day activities. However, in 1883, railroad companies decided to implement four standard time zones across the continent in order to create more precise scheduling and prevent dangerous collisions. This was made possible thanks to the telegraph network, which could provide instant coordination across the distant locations on the railway. This standardization benefited manufacturing, commerce, and finance, propelling the nation toward a more modern world.

Another unexpected benefit was the push the telegraph network gave to women's emancipation. As the network expanded, it created a whole new occupation that was open to women. Women were cheaper to hire, making them the more economical choice for these new telegraph companies. Their hands were often smaller and considered to be better suited for the delicate task of telegraph messaging. During the American Civil War, as men were drafted to the front lines, women took advantage of the increasing demand for operators. It was seen as light, easy work that was more suitable to a woman's aptitude and could provide a temporary income until she got married, which provided telegraph companies with a stable but temporary workforce, meaning they could keep labor costs down. Soon, the job of a telegraph operator was seen as women's work, and it became a place where women could develop new technical skills, form social connections, and find both educational and professional development. This laid the foundation for women's participation in the later labor movements and women's suffrage.

Women working in a cotton mill.[14]

The telegraph also helped to revolutionize journalism in the 19th century, as it modernized reporting and dissemination of news on both sides of the Atlantic. Newspapers, where they existed, had primarily focused on local coverage. Any national or international news might appear weeks after it had occurred. When telegraph cables were laid across the Atlantic and North America, news could be transmitted almost immediately, as correspondents and reporters sent their messages to newsrooms within minutes. Newspaper syndicates, like the Associated Press, pooled resources and were able to maximize the benefits of the technology, and major newspapers started competing for who could publish the latest breaking news.

Legacy of the Telegraph

Samuel Morse achieved his goal of enabling faster communication over long distances so that what happened to him when his wife passed away could be avoided, but his technology had a profound impact on our society, technology, and even language. The examples above are only a few ways in which the telegraph enabled a shift in society during the latter half of the Industrial Revolution; we could fill another book with the ways the telegraph impacted technological developments as well. The popularity of the telegraph led to the formation of professional engineering societies, specialized research workshops, and whole university departments that were dedicated to technological advancements, allowing for major scientific discoveries in later years.

The basic principles that Samuel Morse and Alfred Vail set down pioneered information encoding, signal processing, and data transmission, which we use on a daily basis in the 21st century without thought to their origins. Without the telegraph, we may not have the computers and wireless networks we take for granted today. It is possible to trace a direct line from the encoding process of Morse code to modern ASCII, which is an encoding system that assigns unique numerical values to letters, numbers, and symbols, allowing computers to process text data—it is very similar to Morse's original idea of assigning numbers to popular words in the dictionary. The telegraph and new communication technology facilitated the development of information theory, which forms the technical groundwork for our modern digital world, from the internet to radio to even printing technology!

Aside from the scientific and technological advancements, the telegraph enabled the interconnected system we have for global finance, diplomacy, and work. With the telegraph, companies could begin to expand and remain in constant communication. In order to do so, they created new organizational structures and messaging systems, slowly transforming the world of business from hyper-local to hyper-global. The concept of remote work itself could not have existed before the telegraph since there was no reason to live far away from the place you worked, whether that be as a banker, secretary, or factory worker.

A similar shift in structure affected the financial sector, as the telegraph allowed for the invention of the stock ticker—an instant transmission of stock prices and market information between distant cities. All of a sudden, average investors, whether they lived in New York, London, or a smaller city, could participate in foreign markets and have instant information about their investments. This contributed massively to the prominence of Wall Street and the New York Stock Exchange.

There were, of course, challenges in adopting the stock market. The first few attempts at a transatlantic cable failed, and it was a costly endeavor to get it running again. In fact, every cable that was laid down came with a hefty price tag until companies could start building upon the lines that had been laid down in times of national need, like the American Civil War. That being said, the cost pales in comparison with the impact of the telegraph on our modern daily life. The telegraph was a major leap in transforming communication and daily life, serving as one of the key innovations that propelled the Industrial Age forward until it was eventually surpassed by the invention of the telephone in 1876.

Chapter 8: Child Labor and the Factory Acts

As labor practices shifted and factories dominated the workforce, the people needed to man these places changed. Throughout this book, we have seen how factories needed unskilled workers who completed repetitive tasks day after day as labor conditions got worse and as capitalism took over from cottage industries.

Child labor was already an accepted part of society before the Industrial Revolution. At the time, children were seen more as small adults who were capable of contributing to the family from a young age. The idea of a "protected childhood," with a focus on education and development, was not common, especially among the lower classes. While those from aristocratic backgrounds had tutors in languages, literacy, and other subjects, working-class children saw work as their education. It prepared them for their adult life and was seen as contributing to the home.

The work was either based in the home or on the farm. They often worked alongside their parents with the expectation that the child would one day take over that industry. Children were also employed in wealthier households as domestic servants. Girls, especially, were employed in these households and assisted with cleaning, childcare, or cooking. Boys, on the other hand, were often employed as apprentices, where they learned a particular trade over many years and were expected to care for the master craftsman when he was old and unable to work.

Rather than work for a wage, these children often worked for room and board. They would earn a wage later on in their life once they became a tradesperson or senior domestic servant. The children worked reasonable hours, with breaks for meals that were provided for them by the employer, and they were taught practical skills that would serve them later in life.

There was an umbrella of protection around children since they would either be taken care of by family, their community, or their employer. The nature of this work was always more flexible and family-centric in contrast to the industrialized and unskilled labor that would rise with the advent of the Industrial Revolution. As urbanization and factory work spread, the established system of child labor would change dramatically, sparking debates about children's rights and welfare.

The Rise of Child Labor in the Industrial Revolution

The use of child labor during the Industrial Revolution was a complex phenomenon that changed the economic and social landscape of the leading industrial nations, particularly Great Britain and the United States. As industrialization took hold, factory owners saw the benefits of using child labor to increase their profits. New machinery often had small components or moving parts that were hard for adults to reach when fixing them. Children were able to crawl beneath and through these machines to clean or repair them. For example, Richard Arkwright's water frame had moving spindles that could sometimes clog or tangle. A child could crawl beneath the frame and reach up into the spindles to untangle the cotton yarn more easily than an adult.

As a result, the machines started being built with child labor in mind, with them being built lower to the ground. There were also more machines in smaller spaces. Children were seen as easier to control and discipline than their adult counterparts, making them preferred workers by those who did not want a lot of pushback in their factories.

In the beginning, there was some moral resistance to child labor in factories; however, economic necessity or benefit often overrode those concerns. Poverty-stricken families relied on their children's wages, and factory owners and manufacturers benefited from the cheaper labor and dexterity of children. Reforms against child labor happened much more slowly than the shift toward it.

Family Economics and Child Labor

The shift toward child labor happened quickly as factories sprang up and independent cottage industries died down. By the early 1800s, children under the age of thirteen made up one-third of all workers in the textile industry. But why?

The economics of the home changed drastically with the rise of industrialization, especially for the working class. Homes did not have a single breadwinner, and people no longer relied on a single industry to support their families. Instead, both parents worked, often for long hours and low wages, and children were expected to bridge the gap. It quickly turned into a vicious cycle. Adults were paid a barely livable wage and were faced with the choice of either starvation or sending their children to work. Children were paid even less and provided just enough income to cover the basics. Because factory owners were able to pay children a lower wage than adults, the wages for adults stayed low. Families remained in a position where they had to rely on their child's wages to maintain the household.

Children typically began working between the ages of eight and fourteen, though some started as young as four or five. They surrendered their pay to their parents, who spent it according to the needs of the household. As older siblings became independent, it fell to the younger siblings to continue working to support the household. Education was expensive for these families, so children's attendance at school was inconsistent at best. There was, in a way, nowhere else for the children to go except to work.

Orphaned children often fared an even worse fate. Rather than having their wages go to a family or their own livelihood, they were indebted to the factory for their room and board. In some places, orphans were "bought" by factory owners and forced to sign predatory contracts, though almost all of these children were illiterate and unlikely to know what they were signing. These contracts kept them in the custody of the factory until they were twenty-one years old. The factory owners charged the orphan children for their room and board, and they were housed on the upper floors of the factories they worked. Essentially, they were not working for a wage at all. Some of these children rotated their beds, collapsing in a bunk at the end of their day just as another was getting up to start their shift.

The Risk of Work

The children worked twelve- to sixteen-hour days performing dangerous tasks with few safety measures in place. Their duties varied based on their age and size. In coal mines, young children worked as pickers (like George Stephenson) or as hurriers—with minecarts strapped to their backs, the children would pull coal through narrow tunnels up to the surface of the mines. In textile factories, they worked as scavengers and piecers, picking up loose cotton under moving machinery. Accidents were common, and children were often injured or killed while working with no compensation paid to them or their parents. Older children worked the machines in factories. In cotton mills, they often worked the power looms or spinners, and in coal mines, they picked coal alongside their adult counterparts.

A child hurrier.[15]

This exposed the children to serious health and safety risks from a young age. Those who worked in coal mines were breathing in coal dust, which led to lung diseases later in life. They were also exposed to gas leaks, and there was the constant danger of being crushed under collapsed mines. Children in textile factories didn't fare much better. Machines were packed together in poorly ventilated factories that were kept warm to keep the quality of the threads high. This meant that contagious diseases could sweep through the factory floor at record speeds. Diseases like typhus and smallpox raged, encouraged by the poor sanitation in the mills and living spaces around them. Beyond that, those who worked in cotton mills were also exposed to respiratory diseases from breathing in cotton dust. Children suffered hearing loss from the constant drone of the machines and even chemical exposure from the various dyes and baths.

Factory owners, manufacturers, and merchants all benefited from keeping wages low and employing children at a young age. Unlike the pre-industrial apprenticeships, these children were not taught a skill or trade and instead worked at repetitive jobs in factories until they finally died or became disabled, which often happened at a young age due to health complications. They remained illiterate, poor, and at the mercy of the industry in which they worked. Any dip in trade or the economy resulted in the loss of work, for which there was no protection for children or their parents.

Public Perception and Attempts at Reform

From the beginning, there was some moral resistance to child labor, but the wave of pressure from those who benefited from it overwhelmed any voices that might have stood against them. It wasn't until the 1830s that any meaningful reforms were made, but prior to that, there were some cases and committees presented to British Parliament that made the reforms of the Factory Acts truly take hold.

The Health and Morals of Apprentices Act (some child laborers were called "apprentices," but these roles bore little to no resemblance to trade apprentices) of 1802 was the first legislation aimed at regulating child labor in Britain. This act limited their working hours to twelve per day and required children to have a basic education in reading, writing, and arithmetic. However, the rule was not enforced, and its scope was limited.

The Cotton Mills and Factories Act of 1819 expanded a little bit on the Health and Morals Act; it banned the employment of children under nine years of age in all cotton mills and limited the working hours of those between the ages of nine and sixteen to twelve hours per day. This act was also unenforceable. There was no mechanism or body to check on the many, many cotton mills in Britain and enforce the rules of the act. Unless a factory owner was compassionate enough to comply, the act did not change working conditions. That being said, they do demonstrate that the public was aware of the exploitative nature of child labor and was interested in some kind of reform.

The Sadler Committee Report

In 1831, Michael Thomas Sadler, a member of Parliament from Leeds, introduced a piece of legislation that, once again, proposed limiting the working hours of everyone under the age of eighteen to ten hours per day. There was a heated debate against this, with some arguing that limiting work hours would create an economic crisis in Britain and that purchasers would turn away from British merchants when they inevitably could not meet demand. Parliament agreed that a committee would gather evidence about the working conditions of the factory workers, in particular the children, in order to establish whether Sadler's proposition was necessary. The committee interviewed eighty-nine witnesses, both adults and children, over the course of the investigation.

The initial witnesses were factory workers, who described the brutal conditions of the factories and why their children were sent to work. One witness, a man named Joshua Drake, described it as "Necessity compels a man that has children to let them work."[i] Others were adult workers who had been children when they started working. They described the fourteen- to sixteen-hour workdays, the lack of proper meals, physical abuse, dangerous working conditions, and the pay consequences. One witness, Elizabeth Bentley, described being fined more than she earned if she was a quarter of an hour late. One witness described how he was "sold" to a factory by his mother for fifteen shillings and was beaten when he attempted to escape the factory where he lived and worked.

When these witnesses were fired for participating, Sadler turned to medical professionals who were familiar with the health problems faced by the children who worked in the textile factories. The report was published in newspapers across the country and provoked major public outrage against child labor practices. It directly influenced the Factory Act of 1833, the first meaningful piece of legislation against child labor in industrialized Britain (though it only applied to the textile industry).

---

[i] Sadler, Michael. Evidence Given Before the Sadler Committee. 1832, Hanover College, https://history.hanover.edu/courses/excerpts/111sad.html . Accessed 7 Mar. 2025.

Children working in a textile factory.[16]

Ashley Mines Commission

The Ashley Mines Commission (also known as the Children's Employment Commission) was established eight years after the Sadler Report provoked Parliament to enact the Factory Act of 1833, this time focusing on the welfare of children working in mines. It was created in response to growing public concern, especially after the 1838 Huskar pit disaster, where twenty-six children drowned after a violent thunderstorm caused flooding in the Moorend Colliery. The twenty-six children were trying to climb out of the flooding pit through a day-hole (a ventilation shaft) when a torrent of water swept through and trapped them.

Under the leadership of Lord Anthony Ashley Cooper, the 7th Earl of Shaftesbury, the commission's goal was to investigate the labor of women and children in the coal mines, focusing on their working conditions, wages, and hours. Once again, testimonies were recorded from men, women, and children who worked in the mines, though many were hesitant to testify in fear of losing their jobs.

Women described suffering repeated miscarriages due to the intense physical labor. Many children testified that they did not attend day school (they went to only Sunday school), and they could not read or write. Children described working on their parents' accounts when their parents could no longer work. All of them described suffering from ill health and poor physical development. Young women described working naked or almost naked alongside the adult men because of the heat in the mines.

The vivid accounts, especially those of the men, boys, and girls working alongside each other unclothed, scandalized the very proper Victorian society. The findings of the report led to the Mines and Collieries Act of 1842, which banned women and girls from working underground and prohibited boys under the age of ten from working in mines. As with the Factory Act, this act improved the conditions for some, but it did not solve the problem of poor wages, leaving many families more poverty-stricken than before. Still, it was a major step in the fight for labor rights and set down protections that would be built upon in the years to come.

The work of these commissions and committees was to formalize what everyone in society already knew—that child labor was against the morals of Victorian society and that the working conditions were poor and perpetuated the cycle of poverty among the working class. While they did not solve the problem of child labor on their own, they did bring it to the attention of Parliament and created an undeniable record of the working conditions, setting the stage for the many labor reforms that followed.

The Factory Acts

The Factory Acts were a series of laws in Britain passed throughout the 19th century that regulated the working conditions in industrial settings (textiles, mining, and manufacturing), mostly for women and children. Beginning with the Factory Act of 1833, it established the minimum age for work, limited working hours, and safety standards to protect and preserve the welfare of working women and children. In contrast to the labor movements that would happen in the late 19th and early 20th centuries, the Factory Acts did not initially address wages or working conditions for adult men. They were also driven by the morals of Victorian society, and a few progressive factory owners and members of Parliament, rather than the workers themselves, laid crucial groundwork for the more extensive labor movements that would happen in later years.

Timeline of Labor Legislation in Victorian Britain

1802 Health and Morals of Apprentices Act: This was the first attempt to regulate child labor. It limited the working hours for "apprentices" to twelve hours per day and required basic education for apprentices.

1819 Cotton Mills and Factories Act: This act set the minimum working age to nine years old and limited working hours to twelve per day for children who worked in cotton mills and factories. Like the previous act, this was poorly enforced, and its scope was restricted to the cotton industry only.

1831 Labor in Cotton Mills Act: Building on the Cotton Mills and Factories Act, this act expanded those same measures to wool and silk mills. It maintained the limit of a twelve-hour workday for those under the age of eighteen.

1833 Factory Act: Also known as Althorp's Act, this act prohibited hiring workers under the age of nine and required all employers to have an age certificate for child workers to ensure they met this requirement. It also limited the hours of work. Children aged nine to thirteen could work no more than nine hours per day, and children aged thirteen to eighteen could work no more than twelve hours per day. The children were also not allowed to work at night, and they were required to have at least two hours of schooling each day. The act provided for factory inspectors appointed by the government to enforce the law.

1844 Factory Act: The second of a number of amendments to the Factory Acts, the 1844 act reduced the working hours for children aged eight to thirteen to 6.5 hours per day and required 3 hours of schooling. It also limited women's working hours to twelve per day and decreed that they should not work at night.

1847 Factory Act: Also known as the Ten Hours Act, this limited the working hours for women and children under the age of eighteen to ten hours per day in the textile industries. This amendment was the result of a campaign from Lord Ashley, Earl of Shaftesbury, and John Fielder.

1867 Factory Acts Extension Act: This extended the regulations from the 1847 Ten Hours Act from textile factories to all British factories that employed fifty or more people. It also added the Hours of Labour Regulation Act, which applied the same regulations to workshops (factories or workshops employing less than fifty people). This legislation was put in place to address the number of "sweating systems" that had cropped up to avoid the factory rules. "Sweating" referred to work that had been subcontracted to small workshops where laborers were still unprotected and continued to be exploited.

1901 Factory and Workshop Act: This raised the minimum working age to twelve years old.

In total, there were about twenty different reforms and amendments to the original Factory Act. Some, like the 1860 and 1872 Coal Mines Regulation Acts, were specifically for certain industries, and later laws (like the 1981 Factory and Workshop Consolidating Act) sought to bring them together under one umbrella to create a standard across the country.

The Factory Acts were hard won, as factory owners and manufacturers lobbied against the legislation, often arguing that it would introduce international competition, reduce profits, and result in lost jobs. After the Ten Hours Act, when it became clear that there was little economic effect from regulation, these arguments weakened. Still, factory owners found ways to continue to exploit workers and avoid penalties by hiding underage workers from inspectors, manipulating timekeeping, and using the threat of lost wages or work to keep workers from reporting violations. There were far more factories than inspectors, so exploiting the loopholes in legislation and inspection was easy for those owners who wanted to do so.

Still, the Factory Acts that were passed in the 19th century set the foundation for labor movements and trade unions in the 20th century and set out important standards for labor, including safety regulations that are still the basis of labor rights today. In addition to creating this foundation of labor rights, the Factory Acts contributed to a shift in attitude toward children and the meaning of childhood. Before the Industrial Revolution, childhood was seen as the waiting period before adulthood. Children were expected to work, learn, and prepare for their future lives. Victorian society began to see childhood differently. Children were innocent and needed to be kept safe from adult vices.

The findings from the Sadler Committee and the Ashley Mines Commission served to reinforce this ideal. Journalists and writers like Charles Dickens reframed child labor as a moral failing of industrialization, ultimately helping to secure education for those who didn't have access to it before. The 1870 Education Act was written to "purify" working-class children and, in a way, integrate them into middle-class values and morals. This moralistic attitude, while problematic in some ways, began to reform the idea of childhood into a period of time that should be dominated by education and moral development rather than work, which was beginning to be seen as the adult stage of life.

Chapter 9: Spread of Industrialization

The Industrial Revolution began in Britain, and thanks to the expansive British Empire, the technology and social effects spread throughout all the settled continents. Soon, other countries began to adopt British machines and started their own revolutions.

Industrialization in the United States

The US experienced a similar rate of growth as Britain, driven in part by its abundance of natural resources; a growing labor force, thanks to waves of immigrants and the slave trade; and technological innovations by American inventors.

Samuel Morse was not the only American who invented new technologies. Eli Whitney's cotton gin was a major contributor to the industrialization of the cotton and textile industries. Whitney invented the cotton gin in 1793. It was a mechanical device that was designed to quickly and efficiently separate cotton fibers from their seeds. Raw cotton was fed into a hopper at the top of the machine. It then passed through a compartment containing a series of circular saws mounted on a rotating cylinder. The saws had small teeth that caught the cotton fibers and pulled them through a metal grate or mesh that was too fine for the seeds to pass through. On the other side of the grate, a second cylinder with brushes rotated in the opposite direction, picking up the cleaned cotton fibers from the saw teeth. These were then collected while the seeds fell into a separate container.

This simple machine could process up to fifty pounds of cotton per day, which was a huge improvement over doing it manually, making cotton production significantly more profitable in the American South. Eli Whitney made other significant contributions to American manufacturing as well. He pioneered the idea of interchangeable parts for musket production, laying the groundwork for mass-production techniques in the United States.

Other major figures in the American Industrial Revolution were Samuel Slater and Henry Ford, though their impacts happened at very different times. Samuel Slater is often referred to as the Father of the American Industrial Revolution for his role in bringing British textile technology to the United States. After memorizing the designs of the textile machinery in his hometown of Derbyshire, Slater immigrated to the United States and set up his own textile mill in Rhode Island. Slater modeled his mill after the ones in England, creating Slaterville, a factory town for his mill workers. It was part of a factory system that would come to be known as the "Rhode Island System." Similar to mills in Britain, Slater's mills capitalized on the proximity to water and the import of cotton (though he was importing it from the American South, which was much cheaper) for their success.

Henry Ford, on the other hand, bookmarks Samuel Slater in the timeline of the American Revolution. In 1913, he completely overhauled the manufacturing process and reshaped the modern automotive industry with the moving assembly line. The innovation, in which workers dedicated themselves to constructing one piece of the car as the car automatically moved down a conveyor belt to the next station, increased production and reduced the average build time from hours to minutes. This simple change democratized car ownership. Cars were faster and easier to build, making them more affordable for the average consumer. Ford also introduced the eight-hour workday and five-day workweek. He even introduced a $5 daily salary in 1914. While that seems like a very low wage for us today, in 1914, that was more than double the average wage of a factory worker, allowing them to be able to afford the products they helped manufacture. This helped contribute to the rise of the American middle class.

Expansion into Europe

Britain's growing dominance in territory and industry was not ignored by Europe. In fact, some European nations even sent spies into Britain to gather information about new technologies and manufacturing processes so they could replicate them back home! Eventually, the technology spread naturally through trade and commerce, and countries like France, Germany, and Belgium would find their own strengths in the world of industrialism. As skilled workers left England in search of better opportunities elsewhere, they brought with them knowledge of these new machines. European industrialists worked to reverse-engineer them and develop their own improvements.

Belgium became the first of the European continental countries to industrialize. With its abundant coal reserves and strong banking system, the country was able to invest in itself and grow. By the 1820s, Belgium had established a thriving textile industry and was already expanding into iron production.

France did not rely on coal as Belgium and Britain did. France focused on mechanizing its traditional industries like textiles and luxury goods, and the government invested in infrastructure projects like railways in order to support industrial growth within its territory. Germany's Industrial Revolution took a little longer. It did not begin in earnest until after unification in 1871. The Ruhr region became its hub for coal mining and steel production. Germany invested in its universities through subsidies, encouraging research and advancements in chemistry and engineering.

Overall, the pace of industrialization varied across the continent due to the disparity in natural resources and economies. Southern European countries struggled in comparison, partly because of limited resources but also because of their struggle to build infrastructure, especially in the aftermath of the Napoleonic Wars. Instead, these countries turned to their colonies, focusing on imperial expansion and resource extraction rather than home-grown industries. The American and African colonies became a market for manufactured goods and a resource to make them.

To facilitate the extraction of resources, imperial powers built railways, ports, and communication networks. They imposed European cultural practices that allowed some to benefit from this new trade. Local and Indigenous craft was replaced by the same labor structure that was in place in Europe, though, in some places, indentured servitude took hold as a form of cheap labor.

Eastern Industrialization: The Meiji Restoration

Until 1853, Japan was under a strict isolationist policy that restricted international trade and immigration. Once the country opened up, it embraced a rapid modernization policy in order to catch up to the West and remain a powerful and competitive nation in the East.

The leaders of the Meiji period followed a unifying ideology, *Fukoku kyōhei*, or "enrich the country and strengthen the military." The Meiji government implemented key reforms to centralize power and embark on its own path to industrialization. It abandoned the feudal system for a more centralized government that reflected those of European powers, with an emperor as the figurehead and the Imperial Army replacing samurai-controlled regional forces. In order to keep pace with the rate of industrialization elsewhere in the world, the Japanese established state-run industries and provided subsidies to key sectors, such as cotton, silk, mining, and railways. Silk soon became Japan's biggest export, aiding the country in expanding its mining and manufacturing efforts.

In the 1870s, Japan sent a cohort of aristocrats to the United States and western Europe to observe industrialization and bring back notes of their progress in order to propel society forward after years of isolationism. The government also recruited *oyatoi gaikokujin*—foreigners with industrial expertise who were tasked with helping to guide Japan's Industrial Revolution. The Meiji government encouraged *zaibatsu*—family-owned conglomerates that boosted the nation's industrial production by diversifying and nationalizing their manufacturing, some of which (like Mitsubishi) still exist today.

Japan's effort in industrializing is an example of a government spearheading technological advancements in order to gain an edge in global trade and to progress the society of their nation. In contrast to the West, the Meiji Restoration did not rely on individual inventors or personal enterprise. Instead, the Japanese relied on a centralized government that had the goal of enriching the nation.

Their efforts were not isolated to industry alone. The Meiji government also introduced educational reforms. It made school compulsory for both boys and girls and established an extensive public school system across the country that focused on more Western subjects like mathematics and foreign languages.

Global Impact of Industrialization

This spread of industrialization led to the spread of the same conditions we have reviewed in this book. All over the world, countries experienced urbanization, changes in labor practices, and a gradual shift to workers' rights. There were new opportunities for social mobility and international trade. The global banking system also shifted, reflecting the same system that was in effect in Britain, with local branches connected to an intermediary. The Industrial Revolution had a dual effect; it not only advanced technology and trade, but it also created a more global society. With railways and telegraphs, distant parts of the world were suddenly connected, allowing for an easier exchange of culture.

However, there were negatives with the positives. The global spread of industrialization resulted in a global push toward resource extraction. Coal and iron became valuable commodities, but they are nonrenewable resources. This led nations to dig further and wider to keep up with demand. Industrial processes introduced massive quantities of pollutants into air, water, and soil systems that had never encountered such substances at those concentrations. Factory emissions released carbon dioxide, sulfur dioxide, and other matter that polluted the air and contributed to respiratory illnesses in cities. Industrial waste contaminated waterways with heavy metals and chemicals that poisoned rivers, lakes, and other bodies of water.

The rapid urbanization that accompanied industrialization concentrated populations in cities that were not built to hold them. They lacked the right infrastructure and couldn't adapt fast enough. This created years of unsanitary living conditions and poor waste management, which contributed to illness and a poor quality of life for the working class.

To this day, we are still struggling with the legacy of pollution and environmental degradation that we inherited from the Industrial Revolution. However, recent initiatives could help future generations in combating these effects.

Conclusion

The legacy of the Industrial Revolution continues to shape our world, echoing through time and influencing every aspect of modern life. From the humble beginnings of Jethro Tull's seed drill to the transformative power of Samuel Morse's telegraph, this era of history laid the foundation for the technology that shapes our world today. Its influence is not limited to technology either. We have the Industrial Revolution to thank for our major cities and railways, as urbanization shifted the way of life from domestic agriculture to urban living. This legacy began with the Enclosure Acts and the move toward privatization. The agricultural industry was made more efficient, enabling it to feed more people than ever before. The innovations from the Second Agricultural Revolution snowballed until we arrived at the turn of the 20th century, where food production and daily life were completely separate for most people.

We can see that the Industrial Revolution changed our relationship with work and education as well. As time went on and people became more aware of the dangers of child labor, it caused society to shift its thinking about the meaning of childhood. The morality of the Victorian era and the horrors of child labor created new standards for education and a new vision. The time before a child reached eighteen was seen as an age of innocence, a time for learning and developing a moral structure before they went off into the world and started working.

The Factory Acts and the many laws against child labor that followed led to other labor movements. Workers' rights took a long time to catch up, but it is undeniable that the widespread exploitation of the working class during the Industrial Revolution led to the many protections and trade unions we know today. Social safety nets that we now take for granted, things like retirement, disability benefits, and unemployment protections, can trace their origins to the societal shift of the Industrial Revolution. As the cycle of domestic care was transformed by new labor practices, workers and activists began to fight for institutional protections for the old and vulnerable.

Interestingly, the automation of the Industrial Revolution might have played a role in the emancipation of enslaved people. When inventions like the cotton gin came into widespread use, it lessened the need for manpower since the machine could do the same job with fewer people and was more productive. This led to a reexamination of labor in general—why use a man when you could use a machine? While some were understandably afraid of the consequences of this question, like the Luddites, for example, others questioned the need for practices like indentured servitude and slavery, leading to an examination of the morality of these practices.

Along with the emancipation of enslaved people, women's emancipation and suffrage were advanced by the Industrial Revolution. As women entered the workforce in factories and textile mills, they began to earn their own money. They began to be somewhat independent from their families or husbands, challenging traditional gender roles that kept them at home. Cottage industries revolved around the family unit, and any money earned was filtered down from the head of the household (a woman's husband or other male relative). When women went to work, they earned their own paycheck and were able to begin to control the finances of the home alongside their husbands. The days of complete financial independence were still a long way away, though. A woman could earn money, but it was always significantly less than a man, and if she had a husband or children, that money was expected to go toward running the family household. However, the seed had been planted for future movements that demanded equal rights for women, including equal education and equal financial control. The new society brought about by the Industrial Revolution created a crack in the foundation that women, children, immigrants, workers, and other marginalized people were able to widen with persistent activism and a growing social consciousness.

The effects of industrialization went beyond human society and changed our relationship with the natural world as well. The days of balance and harmony were set aside in favor of the insatiable appetite for natural resources that could be used to power the new world. It took a long time for society to realize its effects, but even early on, the smoke-filled skies over manufacturing cities like Philadelphia and Manchester showed us the first signs of pollution and its negative effects on our collective health. Slowly, writers and activists began to question this unrestrained exploitation of nature and began to advocate for wilderness protection, the two most notable perhaps being US President Theodore Roosevelt, who is known as the "Conservation President" for his work protecting public land, and the poet Henry David Thoreau, whose book *Walden* emphasized the moral value of nature and became a rallying cry for those trying to fight for environmental protections.

The trajectory of technological innovation set humanity on a new path—one of constant innovation and progress that has continued into our contemporary world. Every revolution that came after, from the Digital Revolution to our current Information Revolution, builds upon the framework established back in the 18th and 19th centuries, when steam and iron transformed what humans could do. The Industrial Revolution isn't just a dusty piece of history to look back on. It is an ongoing evolution that has had positive and negative consequences for us to keep working and keep progressing. Learning about the beginning of this pivotal moment in human history gives us some perspective for understanding our current society. The machinery that once transformed raw cotton and wool into cloth or used coal-powered steam to drive a locomotive faster than a horse has evolved into technologies that are reweaving the fabric of human society. By learning and examining how they began, we can see the tapestry of human connection and progress being created right before our very eyes.

Here's another book by Enthralling History that you might like

Free limited time bonus

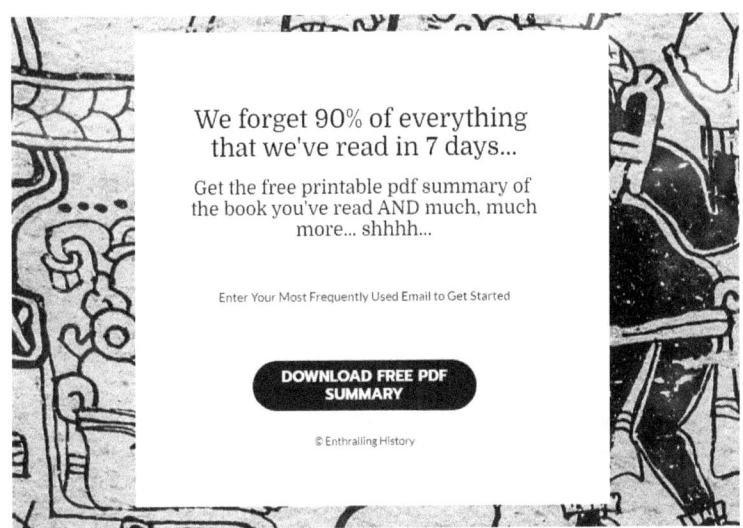

Stop for a moment. We have a free bonus set up for you. The problem is this: we forget 90% of everything that we read after 7 days. Crazy fact, right? Here's the solution: we've created a printable, 1-page pdf summary for this book that you're reading now. All you have to do to get your free pdf summary is to go to the following website: https://livetolearn.lpages.co/enthrallinghistory/

Or, Scan the QR code!

Once you do, it will be intuitive. Enjoy, and thank you!

Bibliography

1: Enclosure Acts and Jethro Tull's Seed Drill

Conner, Clifford D. "The Goose on the Common." Science for the People Magazine, vol. 24, no. 3, Science for the People, www.magazine.scienceforthepeople.org/vol24-3-cooperation/the-goose-on-the-common/.

"James I: The Midlands." Internet Shakespeare Editions, https://internetshakespeare.uvic.ca/Library/SLT/history/james/midlands.html.

"Jethro Tull." American Society of Mechanical Engineers, https://www.asme.org/topics-resources/content/jethro-tull.

"Jethro Tull and the Seed Drill." ThoughtCo, https://www.thoughtco.com/jethro-tull-seed-drill-1991640.

"Norfolk Four-Course System." Encyclopedia Britannica, https://www.britannica.com/topic/Norfolk-four-course-system.

"Progress or Pollution? How British Landscape Painting Captured the Industrial Revolution." Art UK, https://artuk.org/discover/stories/progress-or-pollution-how-british-landscape-painting-captured-the-industrial-revolution.

"The Enclosure Acts: Rural England's Shift to Capitalism." National Bureau of Economic Research, https://www.nber.org/digest/202204/enclosure-rural-england-boosted-productivity-and-inequality.

"The Goose on the Common." Science for the People Magazine, https://magazine.scienceforthepeople.org/vol24-3-cooperation/the-goose-on-the-common/.

2: James Watt and the Steam Engine

"History of Steam Engines." ThoughtCo, https://www.thoughtco.com/history-of-steam-engines-4072565.

"History of the Steam Engine." YouTube, https://www.youtube.com/watch?v=2TtHOkgwrk8.

"How the Steam Engine Changed the World." How Stuff Works, https://science.howstuffworks.com/innovation/inventions/watt-steam-engine.htm.

"James Watt." Encyclopedia Britannica, https://www.britannica.com/biography/James-Watt.

"James Watt: Inventor of the Modern Steam Engine." ThoughtCo, https://www.thoughtco.com/james-watt-inventor-of-the-modern-steam-engine-1992685.

"Steam in the Industrial Revolution." ThoughtCo, https://www.thoughtco.com/steam-in-the-industrial-revolution-1221643.

"Steamcar." Steamcar, http://steamcar.co.uk/.

"The History of the Steam Engine." Victorian Web, https://victorianweb.org/technology/steam/index.html.

"The Rise of the Steam Engine." National Coal Mining Museum, https://www.ncm.org.uk/news/the-rise-of-the-steam-engine/.

"The Steam Engine in the British Industrial Revolution." World History Encyclopedia, https://www.worldhistory.org/article/2166/the-steam-engine-in-the-british-industrial-revolut/.

"The Steam Engine: Evolution and Use." ScienceDirect, https://www.sciencedirect.com/science/article/abs/pii/S0172219007000932.

"Thomas Newcomen: The Steam Engine Pioneer." ThoughtCo, https://www.thoughtco.com/thomas-newcomen-profile-1992201.

"Thomas Savery." Encyclopedia Britannica, https://www.britannica.com/biography/Thomas-Savery.

"Timeline of Steam Power." Wikipedia, https://en.wikipedia.org/wiki/Timeline_of_steam_power.

"Watt Steam Engine." World History Encyclopedia, https://www.worldhistory.org/Watt_Steam_Engine/.

3: Richard Arkwright's Water Frame

"Arkwright's Water Frame." Science Museum Group, https://collection.sciencemuseumgroup.org.uk/objects/co44832/arkwrights-water-frame-1775.

"Arkwright: How Money Conquered Work." Gwydion Williams, https://gwydionwilliams.com/48-economics/037-adam-smith-misleading/arkwright-how-money-conquered-work/.

Cromford Mills History. Cromford Mills, https://www.cromfordmills.org.uk/wp-content/uploads/2021/11/KS-1-2-Topic-Information.pdf.

"Cromford Mills Building 17." European Heritage Awards, https://www.europeanheritageawards.eu/winners/cromford-mills-building-17/.

"Richard Arkwright." Encyclopedia Britannica, https://www.britannica.com/biography/Richard-Arkwright.

"Richard Arkwright." Linda Hall Library, https://www.lindahall.org/about/news/scientist-of-the-day/richard-arkwright/.

"Richard Arkwright." Science and Industry Museum, https://www.scienceandindustrymuseum.org.uk/objects-and-stories/richard-arkwright.

"Science and Industry Museum." YouTube, https://youtu.be/D-6nPEcdvhg.

"The First Factories." Lumen Learning, https://courses.lumenlearning.com/suny-hccc-worldhistory2/chapter/the-first-factories/.

"The History of Cromford Mills." Cromford Mills, https://www.cromfordmills.org.uk/learning/mill-history/.

"The Water Frame." History Mesh, http://historymesh.com/object/water-frame/?story=textiles.

"Water Power and the Cotton Factory: Richard Arkwright at Cromford." Revolutionary Players, https://www.revolutionaryplayers.org.uk/water-power-and-the-cotton-factory-richard-arkwright-at-cromford/.

"Working Woman's Place." History Today, https://www.historytoday.com/working-woman's-place.

4: The Transformation of the Textile Industry

"Cartwright, Edmund." BBC History, https://www.bbc.co.uk/history/historic_figures/cartwright_edmund.shtml.

"Edmund Cartwright." Encyclopedia Britannica, https://www.britannica.com/biography/Edmund-Cartwright.

"Edmund Cartwright." History Crunch, https://www.historycrunch.com/edmund-cartwright.html#/.

"Power Looms in a Textile Mill." World History Encyclopedia, https://www.worldhistory.org/image/17133/power-looms-in-a-textile-mill/.

"Power Looms in the Industrial Revolution." History Crunch, https://www.historycrunch.com/power-loom-invention-in-the-industrial-revolution.html#/.

"Social Change in the British Industrial Revolution." World History Encyclopedia, https://www.worldhistory.org/article/2229/social-change-in-the-british-industrial-revolution/.

"Textile Manufacturing." Lumen Learning, https://courses.lumenlearning.com/suny-hccc-worldhistory2/chapter/textile-manufacturing/.

"The Life of Samuel Crompton." Bolton Lams, https://www.boltonlams.co.uk/homepage/52/the-life-of-samuel-crompton.

"The Textile Industry in the British Industrial Revolution." World History Encyclopedia, https://www.worldhistory.org/article/2183/the-textile-industry-in-the-british-industrial-rev/.

"Work in the Textile Mill." North Carolinapedia, https://www.ncpedia.org/anchor/work-textile-mill.

5: Henry Bessemer and the Mass Production of Steel

"Bessemer Process." YouTube, https://www.youtube.com/watch?v=npp2t3aVZBc&t=5s.

"Bessemer's Volcano and the Birth of Steel." American Scientist, https://www.americanscientist.org/article/bessemers-volcano-and-the-birth-of-steel.

"Henry Bessemer." Encyclopedia Britannica, https://www.britannica.com/biography/Henry-Bessemer.

"Henry Bessemer." Lemelson MIT, https://lemelson.mit.edu/resources/henry-bessemer.

"Henry Bessemer." National Inventors Hall of Fame, https://www.invent.org/inductees/henry-bessemer.

"How the Bessemer Process Changed Steel." Rotabroach, https://www.rotabroach.co.uk/blog/how-the-bessemer-process-changed-steel/.

"Man of Steel: Henry Bessemer." The Chemical Engineer, https://www.thechemicalengineer.com/features/cewctw-henry-bessemer-man-of-steel/.

"Sir Henry Bessemer." Institute of Materials, Minerals & Mining, https://www.iom3.org/resource/sir-henry-bessemer.html.

"Stainless Steel Research Guide." Sheffield City Council, https://www.sheffield.gov.uk/libraries-archives/access-archives-local-studies-library/research-guides/stainless-steel.

"Steel Production." Lumen Learning, https://courses.lumenlearning.com/suny-hccc-worldhistory2/chapter/steel-production/.

6: George Stephenson and the Steam Locomotive

"Anthony Dawson." YouTube, https://www.youtube.com/watch?v=60E3jhwuhng&t=1s.

"Biography: George Stephenson." European Route of Industrial Heritage, https://www.erih.net/how-it-started/stories-about-people-biographies/biography/stephenson.

"George Stephenson." Encyclopedia Britannica, https://www.britannica.com/biography/George-Stephenson.

"George Stephenson." Heritage History, https://www.heritage-history.com/index.php?c=resources&s=char-dir&f=stephenson.

"George Stephenson and the Rise of the Locomotive." The Hopkin Thomas Project, https://www.thehopkinthomasproject.com/TheHopkinThomasProject/TimeLine/Wales/LocomotiveDevelopment/SteamLocomotiveDevelopment.htm.

"George Stephenson: Father of the Railways." Chesterfield Borough Council, https://www.chesterfield.gov.uk/explore-chesterfield/museum/explore-history-with-us/people-of-the-past/george-stephenson-1781-to-1848/.

"History of the Steam Locomotive." Strasburg Railroad, https://mechanical.strasburgrailroad.com/blog/history-steam-locomotive/.

"Science Museum." YouTube, https://www.youtube.com/watch?v=XR4OVtjE3JU&t=1s.

"Stephenson Steam Railway." Stephenson Steam Railway, https://stephensonsteamrailway.org.uk/.

"Stephenson's Rocket: The Rise of the Locomotive." Railway Museum, https://www.railwaymuseum.org.uk/objects-and-stories/stephensons-rocket-rainhill-and-rise-locomotive.

7: Samuel Morse and the Telegraph

"Bound Volume---9 December -9 February 1828." Library of Congress, 1823, www.loc.gov/item/mmorse000009/.

"Did the Telegraph Broaden Women's Sphere?" Engineering and Technology History Wiki, https://ethw.org/Did_the_Telegraph_Broaden_Women's_Sphere%3F

"Electronic Technology: The Telegraph." U.S. House of Representatives, https://history.house.gov/Exhibitions-and-Publications/Electronic-Technology/Telegraph/

"History of the Telegraph." U.S. Department of State: Office of the Historian, https://history.state.gov/milestones/1866-1898/telegraph

"How Samuel Morse Got His Big Idea." Smithsonian Magazine, www.smithsonianmag.com/smithsonian-institution/how-samuel-morse-got-his-big-idea-16403094/.

"How the Telegraph Changed the World." YouTube, https://www.youtube.com/watch?v=2PBB3AMKIgQ.

"How the Telegraph Went from Semaphore to Communication Game Changer." Smithsonian Magazine, www.smithsonianmag.com/arts-culture/how-the-telegraph-went-from-semaphore-to-communication-game-changer-1403433/.

"Impact of the Telegraph." Library of Congress, www.loc.gov/collections/samuel-morse-papers/articles-and-essays/collection-highlights/impact-of-the-telegraph/.

"Invention of the Telegraph." Library of Congress, www.loc.gov/collections/samuel-morse-papers/articles-and-essays/invention-of-the-telegraph/.

"Inventor Samuel Morse Sent the First Official Telegraph from the Supreme Court Chamber." U.S. House of Representatives, https://history.house.gov/Historical-Highlights/1800-1850/Inventor-Samuel-Morse-sent-the-first-official-telegraph-from-the-Supreme-Court-Chamber/

"Milestones: Demonstration of Practical Telegraphy, 1838." Engineering and Technology History Wiki, https://ethw.org/Milestones:Demonstration_of_Practical_Telegraphy,_1838

"Morse's Telegraph in the Capitol." U.S. Senate, www.senate.gov/artandhistory/senate-stories/morses-telegraph-in-the-capitol.htm.

"On This Day: 6th January." Royal Signals Museum, www.royalsignalsmuseum.co.uk/on-this-day-6th-january/.

"Patent History: The Electric Telegraph and Morse Code." Suiter, suiter.com/patent-history-electric-telegraph-morse-code/.

"Samuel Morse." Biography, www.biography.com/inventors/samuel-morse.

"Samuel Morse." Engineering and Technology History Wiki, ethw.org/Samuel_Morse.

"Samuel Morse." Lemelson-MIT Program, lemelson.mit.edu/resources/samuel-morse.

"Samuel Morse and Alfred Vail." Smithsonian Institution Archives, https://siarchives.si.edu/blog/forgotten-history-alfred-vail-and-samuel-morse

"Samuel Morse and the History of the Telegraph." Time, 2016, https://time.com/4307892/samuel-morse-telegraph-history/

"The First Long-Distance Telegraph Message Sent This Day in 1844: 'What Hath God Wrought?'" The Atlantic, 24 May 2013, www.theatlantic.com/technology/archive/2013/05/the-first-long-distance-telegraph-message-sent-this-day-in-1844-what-hath-god-wrought/276226/.

"The Invention of the Telegraph." Digital Library Cornell, https://digital.library.cornell.edu/catalog/chla5743361.

"The Telegraph." Britannica, www.britannica.com/technology/telegraph.

"The Telegraph." Smithsonian Magazine, https://www.smithsonianmag.com/smithsonian-institution/how-samuel-morse-got-his-big-idea-16403094/.

"The Tilt: The Telegraph and 19th-Century Newspapers." The Tilt, www.thetilt.com/content/telegraph-newspapers-19th-century-disruption.

"Time Capsule: 1830-1860." Elon University, www.elon.edu/u/imagining/time-capsule/150-years/back-1830-1860/.

8: Child Labor and the Factory Acts

"1833 Factory Act." The National Archives, www.nationalarchives.gov.uk/education/resources/1833-factory-act/.

"Child Labor." Lumen Learning, courses.lumenlearning.com/suny-hccc-worldhistory2/chapter/child-labor/.

"Child Labor During the British Industrial Revolution." EH.net Encyclopedia, https://eh.net/encyclopedia/child-labor-during-the-british-industrial-revolution/

"Child Labour in the British Industrial Revolution." World History Encyclopedia, www.worldhistory.org/article/2216/child-labour-in-the-british-industrial-revolution/.

"Coal Mining and the Victorians." My Learning, www.mylearning.org/stories/coal-mining-and-the-victorians/236.

"Early Factory Legislation." UK Parliament, www.parliament.uk/about/living-heritage/transformingsociety/livinglearning/19thcentury/overview/earlyfactorylegislation/.

"Factory Acts Overview." UK Parliament, www.parliament.uk/about/living-heritage/transformingsociety/livinglearning/19thcentury/overview/factoryact/.

"Later Factory Legislation." UK Parliament, www.parliament.uk/about/living-heritage/transformingsociety/livinglearning/19thcentury/overview/laterfactorylegl/.

"Michael Thomas Sadler." Britannica, www.britannica.com/biography/Michael-Thomas-Sadler.

"The Victorian Web: Lord Ashley and the Factory Acts." Victorian Web, https://victorianweb.org/history/ashley.html

9: Spread of Industrialization

"Cotton Gin." Encyclopedia Britannica, https://www.britannica.com/technology/cotton-gin.

"DHT." OpenEdition Journals, https://doi.org/10.4000/dht.1340.

"Ford Workday: 8 Hours, 5 Days." Automotive History, https://automotivehistory.org/ford-workday-8-hours-5-days/.

"Henry Ford." History.com, https://www.history.com/topics/inventions/henry-ford.

"History of Europe: The Industrial Revolution." Encyclopedia Britannica, https://www.britannica.com/topic/history-of-Europe/The-Industrial-Revolution.

"Industrialization." Investopedia, https://www.investopedia.com/terms/i/industrialization.asp.

"Second Industrial Revolution." Economipedia, https://economipedia.com/definiciones/second-industrial-revolution.html.

"The Impact of the Industrial Revolution on Society and Economy." The Wow Adventure, https://www.thewowadventure.com/the-impact-of-the-industrial-revolution-on-society-and-economy/.

"The Industrial Revolution in Europe." European Route of Industrial Heritage (ERIH), https://www.erih.net/how-it-started/the-industrial-revolution-in-europe.

"The Industrial Revolution: Henry Ford." Investopedia, https://www.investopedia.com/henry-ford-5225035.

"The Invention of the Telegraph." Digital Library Cornell, https://digital.library.cornell.edu/catalog/chla5743361.

"The Meiji Restoration." Nippon.com, https://www.nippon.com/en/japan-topics/b06904/.

"The Meiji Restoration: Catalyzing Japan's Modernization." Trip to Japan, https://www.triptojapan.com/blog/the-meiji-restoration-catalyzing-japan-s-modernization.

"Who Made America? The Industrial Revolution: Samuel Slater." PBS, https://www.pbs.org/wgbh/theymadeamerica/whomade/slater_hi.html.

"Why the Industrial Revolution Started in Britain." World History Encyclopedia, https://www.worldhistory.org/article/2221/why-the-industrial-revolution-started-in-britain/.

"World History - Origins: Unit 7: Industrial Imperialism." OER Project, https://www.oerproject.com/World-History-Origins/Unit-7/Industrial-Imperialism.

General Resources

"Atlantic Cable Entries." Atlantic Cable, https://atlantic-cable.com/Cables/1852PEI/index.htm, https://atlantic-cable.com/Cables/1856CabotStraitCable/index.htm.

Cambridge University Press. "Industrial Revolution Excerpt." Cambridge University Press, https://assets.cambridge.org/97805218/47568/excerpt/9780521847568_excerpt.htm.

"Hanover College Source." Hanover College, https://history.hanover.edu/courses/excerpts/111sad.html.

"Industrial Revolution." Britannica, www.britannica.com/event/Industrial-Revolution.

"Industrial Revolution." Lawrenceville School Library, https://libguides.lawrenceville.org/c.php?g=533414&p=3649770.

"Industrial Revolution - Research Guide." Taft School Library, https://taftschool.libguides.com/c.php?g=1191731.

Kelly, Martin. "The Industrial Revolution in Europe." ThoughtCo, 5 Oct. 2019, www.thoughtco.com/european-history-industry-4133309.

"Modern History Sourcebook: The Industrial Revolution." Fordham University, sourcebooks.fordham.edu/mod/modsbook14.asp.

Portland State University. "Dissertation on Industrial Revolution." Portland State University, https://pdxscholar.library.pdx.edu/open_access_etds/212/. DOI: 10.15760/etd.212.

"Sessions and Resources - Empire and Industry." The National Archives, www.nationalarchives.gov.uk/education/sessions-and-resources/?time-period=empire-and-industry.

Image Sources

1 https://commons.wikimedia.org/wiki/File:Jethro_Tull_seed_drill_(1762).png
2 https://commons.wikimedia.org/wiki/File:Newcomens_Dampfmaschine_aus_Meyers_1890.png
3 Nicolás Pérez, CC BY-SA 3.0 <http://creativecommons.org/licenses/by-sa/3.0/>, via Wikimedia Commons, https://commons.wikimedia.org/wiki/File:Maquina_vapor_Watt_ETSIIM.jpg
4 Geni, CC BY-SA 4.0 <https://creativecommons.org/licenses/by-sa/4.0>, via Wikimedia Commons, https://commons.wikimedia.org/wiki/File:Spinning_jenny_blackburn.JPG
5 Gregory Deryckère, CC BY-SA 3.0 <http://creativecommons.org/licenses/by-sa/3.0/>, via Wikimedia Commons, https://commons.wikimedia.org/wiki/File:Arkright%27s_Mill_-_Cromford_29-04-06.jpg
6 Pezzab, CC BY-SA 3.0 <http://creativecommons.org/licenses/by-sa/3.0/>, via Wikimedia Commons, https://commons.wikimedia.org/wiki/File:Mule-jenny.jpg
7 https://commons.wikimedia.org/wiki/File:Maudslay_screw-cutting_lathes_of_circa_1797_and_1800.png
8 https://commons.wikimedia.org/wiki/File:Dore_London.jpg
9 https://commons.wikimedia.org/wiki/File:Bessemer_converter.jpg
10 https://commons.wikimedia.org/wiki/File:George_Washington_Wilson.jpg
11 https://commons.wikimedia.org/wiki/File:Opening_Liverpool_and_Manchester_Railway.jpg
12 William M. Connolley (talk · contribs), CC BY-SA 3.0 <http://creativecommons.org/licenses/by-sa/3.0/>, via Wikimedia Commons, https://commons.wikimedia.org/wiki/File:Stephenson%27s_Rocket.jpg

13 https://commons.wikimedia.org/wiki/File:Gallery_of_the_Louvre_1831-33_Samuel_Morse.jpg
14 https://commons.wikimedia.org/wiki/File:Bomullsfabrik.jpg
15 https://commons.wikimedia.org/wiki/File:Coaltub.png
16 Wellcome Collection, CC BY 4.0 <https://creativecommons.org/licenses/by/4.0>, via Wikimedia Commons, https://commons.wikimedia.org/wiki/File: Child_apprentices_in_textile_factory._Wellcome_M0013538EA.jpg

www.ingramcontent.com/pod-product-compliance
Lightning Source LLC
Chambersburg PA
CBHW070336010526
44107CB00004B/527